healing
foods

healing foods

Katherine Wright

The material contained in this book is set out in good faith for general guidance only. Whilst every effort has been made to ensure that the information in this book is accurate, relevant and up to date, this book is sold on the condition that neither the author nor the publisher can be found legally responsible for the consequences of any errors or omissions.

Diagnosis and treatment are skilled undertakings which must always be carried out by a doctor and not from the pages of a book.

This edition published 2014 by Geddes & Grosset,
an imprint of The Gresham Publishing Company Ltd,
Academy Park, Building 4000, Gower Street, Glasgow, G51 1PR, Scotland

First published 2002. Reprinted 2002, 2005, 2006,
2008, 2009, 2010, 2014

Text by Katherine Wright

ISBN 978 1 84205 157 3

Printed and bound in the EU

Introduction

HISTORICAL evidence reveals that the 'doctors' and healers of ancient civilizations were knowledgeable about the health-giving, healing properties of foods. They often conducted their own 'experiments' and made their own observations, adding to a fund of knowledge that was built up over centuries. In many cases, it was probably only the powerful and affluent members of society who were in a position to choose what they ate and able to benefit from this knowledge. Poorer people ate whatever they could gather, grow or kill, regardless of whether the food was good for them or not, with times of plenty alternating with periods of famine.

In the past, knowledge about the healing properties of foods could only be gained through observation. Today, modern analysis and study has been able to unravel the biochemical/cellular action of foods, providing scientific evidence to support the observations of the past. This has proved to be particularly interesting and rewarding with regard to the study of herbs and medicinal plants and a great deal of scientific research continues to be directed towards discovering the healing properties of these foods.

During the 20th century, great advances were made in medicine and science, and for a time it seemed that these held the answers to all human ills. Previously feared infectious diseases were conquered through a combination of vaccination and treatment with new antibiotic drugs. Also, doctors and surgeons were able to harness the products of a second technological revolution (in areas such as robotics, lasers, computers, microsurgery, cryosurgery, advanced diagnostic and scanning equipment, etc.) to treat and cure people in ways that were previously unimaginable. There is no doubt that these advances have made and will continue to make an enormous difference to our health and quality of life. In the event of illness, our chances of survival are much improved and more people than ever before are living to an advanced age.

However, there has also been a growing realization that science and medicine do not have all the answers and that each individual can influence his or her own health through simple lifestyle choices. The most important choice to make is deciding whether or not to smoke as cigarettes remain the principal cause of premature and entirely preventable death in the United Kingdom. Smoking primarily causes death from cancer and heart disease but it is also responsible for many other serious and sometimes fatal respiratory illnesses. Lung cancer, which is responsible for a fifth of all cancer deaths, is almost entirely attributable to smoking.

When it comes to a healthy lifestyle, there are two other areas of equal importance that lie within individual control – diet and exercise. This book deals with diet and, more specifically, looks at the health-enhancing and/or healing properties of a wide range of foods, explaining why these should be included in the daily diet.

There is universal agreement among nutritionists, doctors and scientists about the importance of diet in both the incidence and prevention of disease. It is also accepted that the type of diet prevalent in the UK and many other Western countries is unhealthy and responsible not only for diseases that cause disability and premature death but also for an 'epidemic' of obesity and a steep rise in the incidence of non-insulin dependent diabetes mellitus. Although these facts are well known, many people remain confused about what they should be eating. This is partly due to the barrage of sometimes conflicting advice about food which has been aimed at the public in recent years.

It is hoped that this book will help to throw light on the subject. The first section looks at the different elements in food and their role in the human body. The second section, which forms the main part of the book, consists of an A to Z of health-giving and healing foods, describing their essential properties, giving advice on how much should be eaten and providing cooking methods, where appropriate. The entries mainly cover foods in their essential or natural state rather than products or dishes made from them, although these may be included in the description.

Although the A to Z section includes only those foods that are held to have specific health-enhancing properties, this does not mean that foods that are not included are unhealthy or harmful. It is certainly better to eat some things sparingly and in moderation but, above all, food should be enjoyed. There is little point in eating a particular food, however healthy it may be, if you hate every mouthful. Equally, occasional indulgence is not going to cause any lasting harm. There is common sense in the old adage 'a little of what you fancy does you good!'

Food and the Human Body – Our Nutritional Needs

THE human body needs food to provide energy for all life processes and for the growth, repair and maintenance of its cells, tissues and organs. Food consists of three main groups of substances, carbohydrates, proteins and fats, which are needed by the body in differing amounts. In addition, the body needs fibre, vitamins and minerals. Fibre is derived from plant foods and is essential in promoting good health and in helping to prevent a number of serious, life-threatening diseases. Vitamins and minerals are chemical substances that are contained in food and are needed in small amounts to take part in metabolic reactions within cells. It is best to fulfil vitamin and mineral needs by eating a wide variety of foods but supplements may be helpful in some circumstances.

Carbohydrates
Carbohydrates consist of simple and complex combinations of sugar molecules. The most basic form is glucose. All carbohydrates are eventually broken down by digestive processes into glucose and this is absorbed into the bloodstream and utilized by the body in various ways. This process happens most rapidly if the sugar in

the food is in a simple form. Glucose in the blood may be used immediately, particularly if energy demands are high. For example, athletes often take pure glucose during vigorous exercise.

Starches are more complex carbohydrates built up of long chains of glucose molecules. They take longer to be broken down by digestive processes and hence provide a more gradual and sustained supply of glucose. The body generally contains sufficient reserves of glucose to meet the total energy requirements for one day's activity. If there is a lack of glucose, the body is able to manufacture it in the liver from glycerol (obtained from fats) and amino acids (derived from proteins). Conversely, some excess glucose is converted by the liver into the complex carbohydrate, glycogen or animal starch. This is stored in the liver and in muscle cells and acts as a reserve energy store, which is drawn upon when there is a lack of available glucose in the blood.

Processed foodstuffs, such as sweets, biscuits, cakes, chocolates and sauces, consist mainly of simple sugars. These provide the body with energy molecules in the form of glucose but very little else of nutritional value. People in the UK and other Western countries enjoy these highly palatable foods and often eat them to excess at the expense of more helpful foods. Sustained excess consumption of sugary foods leads to the laying down of body fat and is a leading factor in the development of non-insulin dependent diabetes mellitus, tooth decay and obesity.

There is universal agreement that the most healthy and helpful form of carbohydrate for human beings is starch. Cereals, grains, bread, pasta, potatoes and other vegetables and fruits are not only largely composed of starch but also contain useful fibre, vitamins and minerals. Nutritional experts recommend that complex carbohydrates in the form of starches should make up

Healing Foods

60–70 per cent of overall daily food intake. These should be in the form of wholemeal bread, cereals, whole grains, brown rice, wholemeal pasta and potatoes (especially with their skins) as all of these have a high fibre content. Hence, they are more satisfying and filling than the white varieties of the same foods, and reduce any tendency to overeat. They are of great value in helping to maintain a healthy weight.

Proteins

Proteins are the structural components of the body, forming the basis of cells, tissues and organs. They are composed of amino acids, which are the end products of protein digestion and the form in which proteins are absorbed and utilized by the body. There are 20 basic amino acids, which are usually arranged in lines to make up molecules known as polypeptides. The 20 amino acids can be arranged in a huge number of different ways and most proteins consist of more than one polypeptide chain. There are vast numbers within the human body, each with a unique structure that is drawn from the 'pool' of 20 amino acids. Proteins are used in the body as messengers (e.g. hormones), as catalysts of metabolic reactions (i.e. enzymes), as carriers and for storage.

The body is able to manufacture 12 of the 20 amino acids itself but the remainder, called the essential amino acids, must be obtained from foods. Proteins are widely found in both plant and animal-based foods. Plant sources include beans, peas, pulses, whole grains, nuts and seeds. Red meat, poultry, fish, shellfish, eggs, milk, cheese and dairy produce are the main animal sources. Red meat is usually regarded as first-class protein and is a good source of essential amino acids and iron. However, nutritionists advocate limiting the consumption of red meat to once a week as it can also contain a significant proportion of saturated fat, which is harmful if eaten to excess. Hence, they recommend choosing foods that are high in protein but low in saturated fat, such as pulses, beans, nuts, seeds, fish and poultry breast meat, instead. Protein should only form 10–15 per cent of the total daily intake of food and so only a small amount is needed at each meal. Oily fish, such as mackerel, herring, sardines, salmon, trout, anchovies, pilchards and tuna, are excellent sources of protein. They are also a source of helpful omega-3 oils, which protect against heart disease and some other conditions. Peas and beans provide protein and also help to reduce levels of blood cholesterol.

Fats

Fats are widely found in both plant and animal cells in the form of organic compounds called lipids. They perform many vital functions. They are an important high energy store, having twice the calorific value of carbohydrates, and provide insulation and cushioning. Fats contain fatty acid molecules and may be either saturated or unsaturated, depending upon their chemical structure. Saturated fats are solid while unsaturated ones have a softer, more liquid consistency.

Fatty acids perform three major functions in the human body: they are vital components of the membrane that surrounds each cell and control the passage of substances into the cell and out from it; compounds derived from fatty acids serve as hormones and chemical messengers within and between cells, tissues and organs; and fatty acids are stored inside cells as fuel reserves, which can be broken down when required to release large quantities of energy.

The best-known example of a saturated fat is

cholesterol which is manufactured by the liver from saturated fatty acids. Cholesterol is an essential substance in the body, being a crucial part of cell membranes and involved in the necessary production of steroid hormones and bile salts. However, the body is capable of supplying the necessary amount of cholesterol from a very small dietary intake. In Western countries, the diet is high in saturated fats which are found in red meat, full-fat dairy produce and eggs, but, more importantly, are abundant in processed foods. Also, consumption of helpful, fibre-rich foods, which may bind to cholesterol and remove it from the blood, tends to be low. The result is that too much cholesterol ends up circulating in the blood and if this continues for a long time, there is a high risk of the arteries becoming clogged (atherosclerosis), leading to circulatory and heart disease. An alarming number of schoolchildren in the UK show evidence of early atherosclerosis and this is attributable to a high-fat diet coupled with lack of exercise.

We have seen that fats are essential for human health but in order to prevent disease and to promote good health, they need to be in the right form. Helpful fats belong to the unsaturated group and they exist in two forms: polyunsaturated and monounsaturated.

The polyunsaturated forms include a group that is termed the 'essential fatty acids' because human beings can only obtain them from food. Good sources of polyunsaturated fats are oily fish and various vegetable oils. Oily fish protect against heart disease and studies have shown that people whose traditional diet is rich in these fish, such as the Japanese and Inuit (Eskimos), have a very low incidence of heart disease. Some of these oils also have anti-inflammatory and anti-allergic properties and increased consumption may help sufferers from conditions such as eczema, psoriasis, rheumatoid arthritis and osteoarthritis. Some of the oils are believed to protect against certain forms of cancer (of the ovaries and bowel).

The overall consumption of helpful forms of fat should be in the order of 25 per cent of our daily calorie intake and should not exceed 30 per cent. A diet very low in fat or a no-fat diet is as unhealthy and damaging as eating too much, although in a different way. However, as we have seen, the main problem in Western countries is excess consumption of fat, much of it 'hidden' in processed foods. Three good ways to reduce fat consumption are: to switch to semi-skimmed or skimmed milk and low-fat dairy produce; to avoid highly processed foods; and to choose low-calorie cooking methods such as grilling and steaming.

Fibre

Fibre is found to a greater or lesser extent in all plant-based foods (except for those that have been highly refined by processing). Lack of dietary fibre has been identified as a significant cause of ill-health, being linked with a number of serious illnesses and conditions, not all of which are directly connected with the digestive system. They include bowel cancer, constipation and diverticulosis, and heart and circulatory disease. A lack of dietary fibre also contributes towards the development of obesity, some types of kidney stones, gallstones and non-insulin dependent diabetes mellitus. These conditions are all rare in people whose traditional diet is rich in fibre and largely based on the consumption of plant-based wholefoods.

Fibre, which is also known as roughage, occurs in various forms, depending upon the nature of the source plant. One of the most common forms is cellulose, which is the main constituent of the cell walls of plants. Sources include foods containing wheat bran such as wholemeal flour and bread, wholemeal pasta and also brown rice that retains the husk.

Cellulose is insoluble fibre, which does not break down in water. It is able to bind to water and adds bulk to the waste products of digestion, promoting the efficient operation of the bowel. Other forms of fibre, such as pectins (found in fruits, citrus, vegetables, etc.) and hemicelluloses (found in oat bran, seeds, peas, beans, grains, vegetables and fruits), are water-soluble. They have gel-producing effects and are able to bind to cholesterol. They promote a slower release of food from the stomach, giving more time for nutrients to be broken down and absorbed.

Hemicelluloses are an important source of helpful fatty acids and provide energy for cells lining the colon. They protect against certain forms of cancer. Porridge (from oats) is a well-known form of hemicellulose. Eating porridge at breakfast time has been shown to provide a good source of sustained energy and also to significantly lower blood cholesterol levels.

The health-promoting effects of fibre can be summarized as follows:

1. The presence of fibre necessitates thorough chewing and slows down eating. A feeling of fullness is obtained earlier in the course of a meal and there is less likelihood of consuming too much. Hence, eating plenty of fibre is a good method of calorie control and reduces the risk of weight gain.
2. Fibre helps to retain food in the stomach, promoting a gradual release into the intestine. This decreases the peaking of blood sugar levels which tends to occur during digestion, resulting in a more sustained provision of energy. Avoidance of blood sugar peaks is important in the prevention and treatment of diabetes mellitus.

3. The presence of fibre promotes the release of digestive enzymes and regulatory hormones from the pancreas.
4. Soluble fibre helps to lower blood cholesterol and prevent circulatory and heart disease.
5. Plenty of fibre ensures the efficient working of the bowel and reduces the risk of the development of diverticulae (abnormal pouches formed in the wall of the gut) and haemorrhoids (piles). Efficient working of the bowel helps to promote the speedy elimination of any harmful substances that may have been ingested with the food.
6. Dietary fibre favours the growth of helpful, acid-loving bacteria in the lower gut. These bacteria work to provide the body with helpful fatty acids, some of which have anti-carcinogenic properties.
7. Soluble fibre is a gentle and helpful form of treatment for irritable bowel syndrome (IBS) – a condition that is becoming increasingly prevalent.
8. Some forms of fibre (e.g. mucilages from peas and beans, pectins from fruits, and agar from certain seaweeds) help to eliminate harmful toxins from the body by binding to them and preventing their absorption.

In general, an adult person should try to eat about 30 g of fibre each day. This is easily achieved by eating cereals, wholemeal bread, brown rice, wholemeal pasta, pulses, vegetables, fruits and salads. At least five portions of vegetables and fruit each day are considered necessary for good health.

Some caution may need to be exercised with regard to wheat bran, which can be irritant and play a part in food intolerance and allergy. Taken in excess, pure wheat bran can interfere with the absorption of minerals and vitamins which, in extreme cases, may result in deficiencies. Sufferers from irritable bowel syndrome may need to experiment with eating different foods to find helpful forms of fibre that do not bring on an attack.

Vitamins

Vitamins are a group of organic substances that are required in minute quantities in the diet to maintain good health. They are involved in a large number of metabolic processes, including the growth and repair of tissues and organs, utilisation of food and the functioning of the immune, nervous, circulatory and hormonal systems. Vitamins fall into one of two groups: fat soluble (A, D, E and K); and water-soluble (the B group and vitamin C). A lack of a particular vitamin, especially if prolonged, may result in the development of a deficiency disease. Water-soluble vitamins dissolve in water and cannot be stored in the body but must be obtained from food on a daily basis. Any excess is simply excreted. Fat-soluble vitamins (with the partial exception of D and K) are also obtained from food but any excess can be stored by the liver. Hence, they are needed on a regular basis in order to maintain the body's reserves. However, an excessive intake of some fat-soluble vitamins, especially A and D (which may result from taking too many supplements), is dangerous and can have toxic effects due to accumulation in the liver.

Vitamin A

Vitamin A is fat soluble and plays a vital role in maintaining the health of the epithelial layers of the skin and mucous membranes – the body's barriers against the external environment which provide protection from potentially harmful agents. Vitamin A enhances the immune response by boosting the cells that fight infections and tumours. It is also needed in the manufacture of rhodopsin or visual purple, a light-sensitive pigment that is essential for vision in dim light. Good sources of vitamin A are orange and yellow vegetables and fruits, green vegetables, eggs, full-fat dairy produce, margarine, liver and fish oils.

Several fruits and vegetables contain plant substances called carotenes or carotenoids. Some of these, including beta carotene, one of the best-known examples, are precursors of vitamin A, i.e. they are converted into the vitamin within the body.

Deficiency of vitamin A causes a condition known as night blindness as well as a deterioration in the health of mucous membranes. Symptoms may include dry skin and recurrent respiratory and ear infections. A sustained lack of vitamin A in childhood results in a failure to grow and thrive. Adults who don't receive an adequate supply may suffer from weight loss and debility. Vitamin A is believed to have anti-cancer properties, possibly being protective against cancers of the bowel, bladder, stomach, larynx and lung. A full intake of vitamin A (along with C and E) is believed to be important in the prevention of age-related deterioration in vision.

Vitamin B₁

Vitamin B₁ (thiamine or aneurin) is a water-soluble vitamin. It is involved in carbohydrate metabolism and the production of energy, as well as the healthy functioning of the nervous system and muscles. It plays a part in the mechanisms that combat pain and it may have a role in intellectual functioning. Good sources of thiamine can be found in a wide range of foods, including whole grains, such as brown rice, potatoes, yeast, pulses, green vegetables, eggs, dairy produce, liver, kidney, meat, poultry and fish. A slight deficiency causes digestive upset, sickness, tiredness, and the development of the deficiency disease, beri beri, which occurs mainly among people whose staple diet is polished rice. There is inflammation of nerves, fever, breathing difficulties, palpitations and, in severe cases, heart failure and death.

Vitamin B$_2$

Vitamin B$_2$ (riboflavin) is also water soluble and is involved in carbohydrate metabolism and the provision of energy. Like thiamine, it helps to maintain the health of the skin and mucous membranes and so is involved with the body's frontline defence mechanisms. It is found in a similar range of foods to thiamine. A deficiency may cause a sore, irritated tongue and lips, dry skin and scalp, and possible nervousness, trembling, giddiness and insomnia.

Vitamin B$_3$

Vitamin B$_3$ (niacin, nicotinic acid) is a water-soluble vitamin. It is involved in the maintenance of a healthy blood circulation and also in the functioning of the adrenal glands (hormone-secreting glands located near the kidneys). Good sources include most cereals, nuts, peas, beans, yeast, eggs, dairy produce, dried fruits, globe artichokes, meat, kidney, liver and poultry. A deficiency causes a range of symptoms including sickness, diarrhoea, loss of appetite, dermatitis, peptic ulcer, irritability, depression, tiredness, sleeplessness and depression. In more severe cases, the deficiency disease, pellagra, results, producing the symptoms listed above but with accompanying dementia. Pellagra usually arises in people whose staple diet is maize with an accompanying lack of animal protein or dairy produce.

Vitamin B$_5$

Vitamin B$_5$ (pantothenic acid) is involved in carbohydrate and fat metabolism, the provision of energy, adrenal gland function and maintenance of the nervous and immune systems. This water-soluble vitamin is widely found in all types of food and is also produced within the gut. Deficiency is uncommon but low levels may be associated with poor adrenal gland function which may produce symptoms of tiredness, insomnia, headache, sickness and abdominal pains, especially at times of stress. Low levels of B_5 may also be implicated in the development of osteoarthritis, the most common form of arthritis in older people.

Vitamin B_6

Vitamin B_6 (pyroxidine) is another member of the water-soluble group which is widely found in many foods. It is involved in the metabolism of certain amino acids (proteins) and in the production of disease-fighting antibodies by the immune system. It plays a part in carbohydrate and fat metabolism and in the manufacture of red blood cells. A deficiency is uncommon but low levels may be associated with suppression of the immune system and the development of atherosclerosis (hardening of the arteries).

Vitamin B_9

Vitamin B_9 (folic acid) is necessary for the correct functioning of vitamin B_{12} in the production of red blood cells and in the metabolism of carbohydrates, fats and proteins. It is water soluble and good sources include liver, kidney, yeast, beans, pulses, green vegetables and fruit. A deficiency is quite common and produces degrees of anaemia with symptoms of tiredness, insomnia, forgetfulness and irritability. A good intake of folic acid is important for women who are trying to conceive and for maintaining a healthy pregnancy. Supplements are normally prescribed in these circumstances. A deficiency in folic acid is common in women with cervical dysplasia (abnormality in cells of the cervix, which is a pre-cancerous condition) and in those taking oral contraceptives. In addition, it is commonly deficient in people suffering from some forms of mental illness, depression, Crohn's disease and ulcerative colitis. Elderly people are commonly found to have low levels of folic acid.

Vitamin B complex
Vitamin B complex (biotin) is a water-soluble vitamin involved in the metabolism of fats, including the production of glucose in conditions in which there is a lack of available carbohydrate. It works in conjunction with insulin (the hormone secreted by the pancreas which regulates glucose levels in the blood) although it operates independently. It can be an important substance in the treatment of diabetes. Good sources include egg yolk, liver, kidney, wheat, oats, yeast and nuts. It is also made by bacteria living naturally in the gut. Deficiency is rare in adults but, in young infants, a lack of biotin may be a cause of cradle cap (seborrhoeic dermatitis).

Vitamin B$_{12}$
Vitamin B$_{12}$ (cyano-cobalamin, methyl-cobalamin) is necessary for the correct functioning of folic acid. It is important in the production of genetic material and in the maintenance and operation of nerve fibres. It is also involved in the production of red blood cells and in other cell functions as well as the metabolism of proteins, carbohydrates and fats. B$_{12}$ is a water-soluble vitamin derived from animal sources, such as egg yolk, dairy produce, meat, liver, kidney and fish, but it is often added to (fortified) breakfast cereals. Blood levels of B$_{12}$ are often low in people suffering from Alzheimer's disease and some other forms of psychiatric illnesses. Deficiency causes anaemia but often this is due to a faulty absorption of the vitamin rather than dietary lack. Absorption depends upon the release of certain secretions in the

stomach. If this mechanism is defective, it may result in pernicious anaemia which is cured by injections of B12 directly into the bloodstream. Prolonged dietary deficiency of B12 may result in degeneration of the nervous system possibly producing symptoms of neurological damage and behavioural changes. There may also be symptoms associated with anaemia such as pallor, tiredness and heartbeat irregularities.

Vitamin C

Vitamin C (ascorbic acid) plays a vital role in the maintenance of cell walls and connective tissue and so is essential for the health of blood vessels, skin, cartilage, tendons, ligaments and all the body's lining surfaces. It promotes the uptake and absorption of iron and is crucially involved in the effective operation of the immune system, since it has anti-infection properties. It promotes wound repair and supports the function of the adrenal glands, especially at times of stress. It is also involved in the metabolism of fats and in the control of cholesterol, thereby helping to reduce the risk of arterial disease. Low levels of vitamin C are common in people suffering from a range of disorders, including cataracts, asthma, Crohn's disease and gum disease. The vitamin is water soluble and unstable, hence it is degraded if foods are kept near or subjected to heat, light or cooking. The best sources are fresh fruit and vegetables. A prolonged and severe deficiency of vitamin C causes the development of scurvy, which produces a wide range of symptoms and is ultimately fatal. Full-blown scurvy is rare in Western countries but slight symptoms, due to a low dietary intake of the vitamin, are occasionally reported. Vitamin C may protect against infections, certain cancers, heart disease and some other conditions since it is known to possess antioxidant properties and can help to combat free radical damage.

Healing Foods

Vitamin D
Vitamin D is a fat-soluble vitamin, one form of which is produced within the body by the action of sunlight on the skin. Vitamin D is vital in the control of blood calcium levels. It promotes the absorption of the mineral from food, ensuring that there is a good supply for the growth and repair of bones and teeth. It also facilitates the uptake of phosphorus, which is also vital for the health of teeth, bones and muscles. Good dietary sources of the vitamin include oily fish, eggs, liver, dairy produce and fortified foods such as margarine and breakfast cereals. A slight deficiency causes tooth decay, softening of the bones, muscular cramps and weakness. People from ethnic communities in the UK can be at risk if they cover up completely and eat a traditional diet that is low in the vitamin. Severe and prolonged deficiency results in rickets in children and osteomalacia in adults. Both of these conditions are characterized by soft bones that bend out of shape, causing deformity and risk of fractures. Levels of vitamin D are often found to be low in people suffering from Crohn's disease and ulcerative colitis. Vitamin D is converted by the liver into a more potent form and, in some cases, it appears that it is this mechanism which is at fault rather than dietary deficiency.

It is not advisable to take supplements of vitamin D on its own, except under medical supervision, as this is one of the vitamins that can have toxic effects in high doses. People with normal exposure to the sun manufacture enough storable vitamin D to last for one year, in addition to that obtained from food.

Vitamin E
Vitamin E consists of a group of fat-soluble compounds called tocopherols, which are widely found in a range of foods. Good sources include nuts and seeds,

vegetable oils, green vegetables, eggs, whole grains, cereals, pulses, soya products and margarine. Vitamin E is involved in maintaining the health of red blood cells and cell membranes and in resisting infection. It also plays a part in blood clotting. It has proven antioxidant properties and is believed to be protective against atherosclerosis, some cancers, stroke and heart disease. Deficiency is rare but low levels of the vitamin may cause unhealthy skin and hair, and be a contributory factor in some other disorders.

Vitamin K
Vitamin K (menadione) is a fat-soluble vitamin which is essential for blood clotting. It is manufactured by bacteria naturally present in the large intestine. It is also found in liver, kidney, green vegetables, wheatgerm, eggs and seaweed. Deficiency is rare in healthy people but has been reported in those suffering from disorders of the digestive system such as ulcerative colitis and Crohn's disease. It may also occur as a result of taking large doses of antibiotics over a period of time as this tends to disrupt the natural bacterial balance of the gut. Symptoms include nosebleeds and bleeding beneath the skin.

Vitamins have many functions and properties that are essential for the maintenance of good health, prevention of disease and for healing. It is best to fulfil vitamin needs by eating a wide variety of foods but supplements are helpful at certain stages in life and for people whose state of health might make them vulnerable to deficiency.

Minerals
Minerals are found in rocks and metals but are also present in all living things. They play a vital part in many metabolic processes. Some minerals, notably calcium

and phosphorus, are present in significant amounts in the human body, concentrated mainly in bones and teeth. Others, such as iron, iodine, sodium and potassium, occur in extremely small but vital quantities. Minerals that are only needed in minute amounts are called trace elements and, as with vitamins, deficiency can cause a disease that produces a particular set of symptoms that may develop over a prolonged period. The effects of deficiency may be quite complex in some cases. They may arise as a direct result of dietary insufficiency or because of a lack of absorption of the mineral or due to some other dysfunction within the body.

Minerals are involved in many metabolic processes, both directly and indirectly. Some have antioxidant effects while others are necessary for the function of vitamins, hormones and enzymes (substances within the body that bring about chemical reactions). The importance of minerals has been increasingly recognized in recent years although their role is perhaps less well known than that of vitamins.

Sodium
Sodium is obtained from the diet in the form of common salt (sodium chloride). It is essential for the correct functioning of nerves and as a vital constituent of cellular and tissue fluids. The minute amount needed is readily obtained from natural foods, most of which contain traces of salt. No additional salt needs to be taken. However, the Western diet relies heavily on processed foods that contain much added salt, and this can cause serious health problems. These include heart and circulatory disease, high blood pressure and kidney disorders. The risks of developing these disorders can be reduced by simply not adding salt to food during cooking or at the table, and avoiding eating too many

processed foods. The taste for salt is an acquired habit that, with a little perseverance, can be broken. Try adding herbs and spices instead of salt to food for a different flavour. If you eat a salty meal, drink one or two glasses of water to dilute the effects and ease strain on the kidneys.

Potassium

Potassium is a vital component of cell and tissue fluids and is essential for nerve function. The balance between potassium and sodium levels in body fluid may be quite significant in the development of some diseases and conditions. For example, low potassium/high sodium ratios are a factor in the development of high blood pressure and stress. A deficiency in potassium causes appetite loss and sickness, thirst, muscle weakness and neurological disturbance. In severe and rare cases, there may be unconsciousness and coma. A normal varied diet should contain sufficient amounts of potassium, although levels are often low in highly processed foods.

Calcium

Calcium is present in significant amounts in the human body, forming about two per cent of the total mass, almost entirely concentrated in the bones and teeth. Calcium is essential for the growth and repair of the skeleton and teeth. It is especially important for growing children and young people to eat foods that contain a plentiful supply. Women are in particular need of calcium when pregnant, and during and after the menopause. Vitamin D is necessary for the uptake and utilisation of calcium and the relationship between them is quite complicated. Hence conditions such as osteoporosis (thinning and weakening of the bones) may not always be caused by a dietary lack of calcium but be related to low levels of stomach secretions and the most potent form of vitamin D.

A deficiency in calcium, which is uncommon in people who eat a varied diet and are in general good health, causes rickets in children and osteomalacia in adults (see vitamin D). Calcium-rich foods include milk and dairy produce, fish, flour, bread and fortified cereals.

Iron
Iron is an essential component of haemoglobin, the respiratory compound in red blood cells which transports oxygen from the lungs to all the body's tissues and organs. Iron-rich foods include red meat, liver, kidney, egg yolk, cocoa, nuts, green vegetables, dried fruits, pulses, fortified flour and cereals. Iron is more easily absorbed from meat but its uptake is also enhanced by eating plenty of vitamin C. A deficiency causes anaemia, producing symptoms of tiredness, pallor, feeling cold, shortness of breath, dizziness. Other possible symptoms include irregular heartbeat, swelling of the ankles and weight loss. However, anaemia can also result indirectly from causes other than a dietary lack of iron. Slight anaemia is quite common, especially among women, and frequently goes undiagnosed. Iron supplements are usually given to anyone medically diagnosed with anaemia and the mineral is also routinely prescribed for pregnant women.

Phosphorus
Phosphorus is present in the body in considerable amounts, accounting for about one per cent of total weight. It is concentrated in the bones and teeth, in which it plays a vital role in growth, repair and maintenance. Phosphorus is also essential in energy metabolism and muscular activity and in the function of

certain enzymes. It affects the absorption of other elements and compounds from the small intestine. The body's supply is totally renewed every two to three years. It is widely found in many foods, especially those of animal origin, and so deficiency is rare. In Western countries, there is a greater risk of over-consumption of phosphorus rather than deficiency, because so many animal products are eaten at the expense of plant-based foods. Too high an uptake of phosphorus can reduce or prevent the absorption of iron, calcium, zinc and magnesium. This may also be a factor in the incidence of osteoporosis and some other disorders.

Magnesium
Magnesium is required for the growth, repair and maintenance of bones and teeth, the correct functioning of muscles and nerves, and for metabolic processes involving certain enzymes. It has a role in the function and activity of vitamins B_1 and B_{12}. Magnesium is found widely in many foods, including green vegetables, cereals, whole grains, meat, milk, dairy produce, eggs, shellfish, nuts and pulses. Deficiency is rare in people who eat a normal, varied diet. When it does occur, it causes anxiety, insomnia, cramps, trembling, palpitations and loss of appetite and weight. Low levels of magnesium may be a factor in the development of a number of disorders and conditions, including osteoporosis and high blood pressure.

Iodine
Iodine is essential for the correct functioning of the thyroid gland and is present in two vital thyroid hormones that are responsible for the regulation of metabolism and growth. It is present in high concentrations in seaweed, seafoods, and vegetables and fruits grown on iodine-rich soil. Animals that have

grazed on plants growing on iodine-rich soil incorporate the mineral into their muscles, producing iodine-rich meat. Deficiency is rare because iodine is added to table and cooking salt, and staple foods such as bread and cereals. If it does occur, it results in goitre in which the thyroid gland enlarges, producing a lump in the neck, and causing symptoms of lowered metabolism, weakness and weight gain. Iodine deficiency combined with hypothyroidism may be implicated in some cases of fibrocystic breast disease.

Manganese
Manganese is essential for the activity of many enzymes and metabolic reactions. It is involved in nerve and muscle function, and in the growth and repair of bones. It is a co-factor in a vital enzyme reaction of glucose metabolism and some people with diabetes mellitus and rheumatoid arthritis have been shown to be deficient in the mineral. It is also necessary for the activity of an enzyme called manganese superoxide dismutase, which has important antioxidant properties. Manganese is widely found in many foods but is especially abundant in whole grains, nuts, cereals, avocados, pulses and tea. Deficiency is normally rare.

Copper
Copper is involved in the activity of many enzymes and metabolic functions, as well as the production of red blood cells and connective tissue. It is also necessary for bone growth and repair. It is involved in the metabolism of fats and hence in the fate of the body's fuel reserves. The zinc-copper balance has been demonstrated to be important in the development of some disorders, as the two minerals may 'compete' with one another to a certain extent. A deficiency is uncommon but it may be a factor in the development

of arterial disease and osteoarthritis. Deficiency reduces the number of white blood cells, hence lowering immunity. It may cause diarrhoea and changes in the condition of the hair. Copper is widely found in many foods and sources that are especially rich in the mineral are shellfish, nuts, liver, kidney and cocoa. A dietary lack is normally rare.

Chromium
Chromium is important in a range of metabolic activities, particularly the processing and storage of sugars and fats. It is involved in the activity of insulin, in glucose tolerance in diabetes, and in the function of the immune system. It is also necessary for the correct functioning of the voluntary muscles that move the bones and joints. Chromium is found in many whole and unrefined foods, including wholemeal flour, whole grains, cereals, brewer's yeast, nuts, meat, liver, kidney, vegetables, mushrooms and fresh fruit. A deficiency may cause irritability, depression and forgetfulness but is usually rare in those eating a normal, varied diet.

Sulphur
Sulphur is involved in amino acid metabolism and the manufacture of proteins. It forms an important element of the structural components of the body – bones, teeth, skin and nails. Good sources include meat, liver, garlic, onions, nuts, brewer's yeast, fish, dairy produce and eggs. A deficiency is not normally reported.

Strontium
Strontium is similar in composition to calcium and is also found concentrated in bones and teeth. The mineral is naturally found in milk and dairy produce and helps to ensure the strength of bones and teeth. Deficiency is rarely reported.

Healing Foods

Boron
Boron is thought to be involved in the utilisation of calcium, the activity of vitamin D, and the action of the female hormone, oestrogen. It is thought to be necessary for the conversion process of vitamin D into its most potent form which takes place within the kidneys. It is plentiful in fresh fruit and vegetables, and deficiency is not usually reported.

Selenium
Selenium has become well known in recent years for its powerful antioxidant activity, especially when combined with vitamin E. It is also involved in the functioning of the immune system and liver. It is believed that many people have an insufficiency of this important mineral. The best food sources include Brazil nuts, whole grains, cereals, shellfish, some sea fish, egg yolks, kidney, liver, garlic, radishes and yeast. Selenium is believed to be protective and helpful in the prevention and treatment of a variety of disorders. It is one mineral that may be usefully taken as a supplement.

Zinc
Zinc is essential for the activity of numerous enzymes and is widely involved in metabolic processes. It is necessary for the utilisation of vitamin A and is vital in immune system functioning. Zinc has anti-viral properties, is involved in the healing of wounds and carries out important antioxidant activity. It plays an essential role in insulin metabolism and the control of blood sugar levels. Deficiency has wide-ranging effects, including poor growth and retardation of intellectual faculties, and slow wound healing. Deficiency is common in people suffering from a number of disorders including Crohn's disease, gum disease and under-active thyroid gland. It is believed to increase susceptibility to

viral infections and may be implicated in the development of non-insulin dependent diabetes mellitus. Zinc is widely found in many foods but especially good sources are shellfish, egg yolks, liver, meat, whole grains, wholemeal flour, cereals, seeds and nuts.

Free radicals and antioxidants

Free radicals are naturally occurring, unstable compounds that are highly reactive due to the nature of their atomic structure. They are readily able to attach to and destroy useful molecules within the body and to damage cells. The majority of free radicals are produced within the body as a result of normal metabolism. Among the most potent are toxic oxygen molecules. These are able to oxidize useful agents within the body, including enzymes and other proteins, but also DNA, the genetic material of life itself. In fact, it is estimated that each human cell is assaulted by several thousand free radical attacks each day. Fortunately, the body has defence mechanisms that can be employed to counter these attacks and to repair the ensuing damage. Defence and repair mechanisms work most effectively in youth. One of the main theories about the ageing proposes that over time the rate of free radical damage gradually overwhelms these mechanisms leading to a general accumulation of adverse effects.

Most important among the body's defences are a large, varied group of naturally occurring substances known as antioxidants. The body produces a number of its own antioxidant enzymes but many food substances also possess powerful antioxidant activity. It is impossible to prevent the production of free radicals within the body, but it is possible to ensure that the diet contains plenty of natural antioxidants. These are particularly abundant in fruit and vegetables. Some of the better known antioxidants are described below as well as under the appropriate individual entries in the A to Z section.

Other healing food substances

In recent years, attention has been increasingly focused on a number of 'super' food substances, which appear to have particular health-enhancing properties. Other substances continue to be studied and researched, and so the list is likely to become longer as time goes on.

Carotenes

Carotenes are naturally occurring organic substances containing cartenoids, the orange, yellow or red pigments that are quite widely found in plant and some animal tissues (e.g. egg yolk, milk fat). About 40 to 50 of the cartenoids that have been studied are precursors of provitamin A and can be converted into vitamin A. Also, many carotenes, of which the best known example is beta carotene, have demonstrated potent antioxidant activity. Carotenes are naturally deposited in body tissues and in the thymus gland, an important organ of the immune system. A growing body of evidence suggests that the concentration of carotenes within the body, along with naturally occurring antioxidant enzymes, are factors that affect the lifespan of mammals. The levels of these substances decline with age but it may be that those who are longer-lived are able to maintain higher concentrations in their tissues. Eating a diet rich in carotenes raises the level of these important substances and increases antioxidant capability. The best sources are carrots, squashes, pumpkins, green, leafy vegetables, beets, sweet potatoes (yams) and other coloured vegetables.

Flavonoids

Flavonoids are a group of naturally occurring plant pigments that are widely found in fruits and green vegetables. They are the most potent of known antioxidant substances, having the ability to counteract free radicals, and also possess other properties as well. Flavonoids appear to have anti-cancer, anti-viral, anti-allergic and anti-inflammatory properties, and some also have hormonal-type activity. They are protective of the heart, circulation and skin. It has been discovered that certain flavonoids appear to possess particular affinity with certain tissues. Several thousand flavonoids have been identified and studied, particularly those from plants and herbs that have a long history of traditional, medicinal use. Their efficacy is tending to be proved rather than disproved by scientific scrutiny.

Flavonoids form a very broad group of substances that have wide-ranging effects. The anthocyanidins are particularly important. They are found in highly coloured berries, especially cranberries, bilberries, cherries, blackcurrants, strawberries, raspberries and grapes. These fruits should be eaten as frequently as possible – at least once a week. The largest group of flavonoids are the isoflavones, some of which have natural hormonal activity and can be useful in the treatment and prevention of disorders. Others inhibit the formation of blood capillaries. The latter property is exciting interest in the treatment of some cancers as it is hoped it may be possible to inhibit tumour growth by cutting off blood supply. Isoflavones have natural antioxidant properties, support the immune system and help in the repair of genetic material (DNA). They are naturally found in highly coloured vegetables, seeds, pulses, red wine, nuts and soya produce.

Flavonoids are a huge group of substances with a wide range of properties. Other foods that contain them include citrus fruits, apples, mangoes, pomegranates, tomatoes (including cooked sauces and pastes), herbs (e.g. thyme, marjoram, basil, oregano), garlic, onions, tea, green tea, and fruit and vegetable juices.

Glutathione
Glutathione is a naturally occurring antioxidant, manufactured within the body from certain amino acids. It is believed to be another substance that may be involved in determining the lifespan. While levels naturally decline with age, those who are longer lived appear to maintain a higher concentration of the substance in their blood. Fresh fruit and vegetables, including carrots, tomatoes, broccoli, potatoes, spinach, asparagus, avocado pears and watermelon, are good sources. Glutathione is also found in red meat. It is, however, a substance that is easily destroyed by cooking, and so is best obtained from foods that can be eaten raw.

Co-enzyme Q10
Co-enzyme Q10 is a naturally occurring antioxidant enzyme which is found in almost all human cells and tissues. It plays a vital role in energy metabolism. It is believed that it may help to protect the heart and immune system and has proved useful in the treatment of Alzheimer's dementia. Natural levels of this enzyme decline with age. Good food sources include liver, kidney, soya produce, green vegetables (especially spinach and alfalfa), nuts, yams and oily fish.

Carnosine
Carnosine is a protein compound comprising two amino acids, which is naturally found in muscles, the brain and nervous system, and the lens of the eye. It is a substance that is attracting a great deal of attention from

those engaged in research into ageing, and it has been found to have some truly remarkable properties. Carnosine is a potent antioxidant, which seems to boost activity against free radicals in a number of different organs, including the brain, heart, stomach and liver. It boosts muscle activity during hard exercise and increases the active 'lifespan' of certain cells of the immune system. It also supports the function of the immune system in several other ways and appears to be able to protect the brain from some of the damage associated with Alzheimer's disease. During ageing, there is a build up of abnormal, cross-linked proteins that are no longer able to carry out their proper function. In addition, damaging by-products, known as AGEs, accumulate, and these two processes are believed to be implicated in the development of a number of serious disorders. Carnosine appears to be able to inactivate some of the biochemical pathways that cause cross-linking and the production of AGEs, and hence it helps to protect the body against their potential damaging effects. It is also active against some toxins that may find their way into the body. It possesses the ability to bind to them (chelation), converting them into a harmless form which can be eliminated. In laboratory experiments, human fibroblast cells were 'rejuvenated' when treated with carnosine, which increased their longevity by 20 per cent. Good sources of this substance are lean red meat and poultry.

Phospholipids
Phospholipids are naturally occurring, organic substances containing two fatty acids and phosphate. They are important constituents of cell membranes. One of the most familiar is lecithin, which, along with a related compound, phosphatidyl choline, has beneficial effects on the brain, nervous system and skin. It helps to control

levels of blood cholesterol and promotes the absorption of some vitamins. Good food sources of phospholipids are soya produce, corn, nuts, wholewheat, wheatgerm, egg yolk and liver.

A to Z of
Healing Foods

A to Z of
Healing Foods

Aduki beans

Description: a small, red, dried bean belonging to the pulses group. They are grown in China and Thailand and are used in both savoury and sweet dishes in Eastern cookery.

Properties: a good source of vegetable protein, starch and insoluble and soluble fibre. They contain vitamins (especially the B group and E) and minerals (particularly iron) and are extremely low in fat.

Health benefits: a major source of useful protein for vegetarians when combined with other plant-based foods (e.g. cereals, whole grains and nuts). The high content of insoluble fibre promotes regular bowel habits and may help to protect against cancer of the colon. High content of soluble fibre may help to lower blood cholesterol levels. The starch content provides useful, slow-release energy, avoiding peaks of blood glucose, which is helpful in the control and possibly the prevention of diabetes. Low fat and high fibre/starch content means that they can be eaten freely without risk of weight gain. They contain vitamins and minerals that are essential for good health.

Cooking/serving methods: see PULSES. Aduki beans are ideal in curries and rice dishes and they can be used as a substitute for minced beef in vegetarian versions of

dishes such as shepherd's pie, moussaka, lasagne, etc.
Disadvantages: may cause intestinal wind.

Alfalfa (lucerne) see **bean sprouts**

Allspice
Description: a spice made from the dried, ground-up
berries of an evergreen tree that grows in the
Caribbean and is a member of the Myrtle family. It
tastes like a blend of other aromatic spices –
cinnamon, nutmeg, cloves, juniper – hence the name,
allspice.
Properties: contains the active ingredient, eugenol, which
is found in the volatile oil derived from the fruit and
other parts of the plant. It has medicinal as well as
culinary uses.
Health benefits: the oil in the spice is said to aid
digestion by boosting the activity of trypsin, an
important enzyme, which breaks down food in the
small intestine. Allspice may help to relieve
gastrointestinal wind. In addition, allspice oil (rather
than powdered spice) can be used, sparingly, to
relieve toothache as it has local anaesthetic and
analgesic properties.
Cooking/serving methods: used as a spice to add flavour
to cakes and other sweet and savoury dishes. It can
also be drunk as a medicinal 'tea' and is used in the
Caribbean to relieve colds, menstrual symptoms and
digestive pains. To make the 'tea', add two teaspoons
of allspice powder to a mug and fill with boiling
water. Steep for 10 minutes, strain the liquid and
drink, with or without added sugar. Do not drink
more than three mugs per day.
Disadvantages: normally none associated with the spice.
However, the concentrated oil must be used with
care and should not be swallowed. The oil can also

cause an allergic skin response in people who have eczema or other sensitive skin conditions.

Almonds
Description: flattened, oval-shaped nuts in a brown, papery skin. They are available in this form, blanched with their skins removed and as flakes or ground to a constituency like coarse flour. They have a sweetish flavour and characteristic aroma. Almond trees grow in the British Isles.

Properties: a good source of useful protein for vegetarians when combined with other plant-based foods (e.g. cereals, whole grains and pulses). They are high in fat but in useful, unsaturated form, and contain essential fatty acids. Almonds also contain valuable vitamins (especially the B group and E) and minerals (particularly potassium, phosphorus, copper and iron).

Health benefits: a versatile alternative to animal protein, containing essential vitamins and minerals that protect health. Almonds are used in herbal medicine for digestive and kidney complaints.

Cooking/serving methods: they can be added to savoury dishes or used ground to make nut roasts/cutlets, etc. Flaked nuts are often toasted and used as a topping. The nuts are most often used for making cakes and biscuits, and ground almonds are used for marzipan.

Disadvantages: must only be eaten when mature and ripe – immature nuts can contain substances that produce poisonous hydrogen cyanide, which gives off a distinctive 'bitter almonds' scent. Like most nuts, almonds are high in calories and are best eaten sparingly.

Anchovies
Description: small fish that are available tinned, usually in oil or brine.

Anise

Properties: a good source of essential omega-3 fatty acids, protein, vitamins (A, B$_{12}$ and D) and minerals (iron and selenium).

Health benefits: omega-3 fatty acids protect against heart disease and some other conditions. Anchovies contain vitamins and minerals that are essential for good health and the prevention of disease.

Cooking/serving methods: available cooked and ready to eat – on toast or with salad. Anchovies can also be incorporated into a number of savoury dishes, e.g. as a topping for a pizza.

Disadvantages: they often have a high salt content, especially if canned in brine. If they are canned in vegetable oil, their calorie content is high.

Anise

Description: the anise or aniseed plant is native to Egypt, Crete and Western Asia but it is widely cultivated, e.g. in Central Europe and North Africa. The spice, derived from the seeds, has been used for thousands of years and has a distinctive flavour resembling liquorice. Both seeds and fruit are used in herbal medicine.

Properties: contains active, volatile substances that impart a distinctive flavour to foods.

Health benefits: may relieve indigestion and wind. Anise is used in herbal medicine to treat digestive complaints, coughs, chest infections, catarrh, bad breath and epilepsy.

Cooking/serving methods: used as a spice to flavour cakes, biscuits and some savoury dishes. Anise is used commercially to flavour sweets, drinks (e.g. Greek ouzo), toothpaste, breath sweeteners, air fresheners, etc.

Disadvantages: none reported.

Antioxidants
  Natural substances present in some foods, which are able to counteract the damaging effects of free radicals (see entry in introductory text p.31)

Apples
Description: familiar and popular fruit, of which around 50 or more varieties are grown in Britain, although very few of them commercially. Most eating apples sold in Britain are imported from France, New Zealand, USA, etc. Bramley apples may be imported or home grown and are used in cooking.

Properties: a good source of vitamins (especially C) fruit sugar (fructose), fibre and minerals. They are considered to be an excellent, nutritious, natural snack. Apples have both culinary and medicinal properties.

Health benefits: contain natural antioxidants, provide slow-release energy and promote regular bowel habit. Apples may relieve indigestion and constipation and in herbal medicine are used to treat kidney stones and liver complaints. Stewed apples may be used to relieve sickness and diarrhoea. Poultices made from apples are used to treat skin inflammation and eye problems.

Cooking/serving methods: usually eaten in their fresh, natural state or stewed to make pies or puddings. They can also be dried, as slices or rings, which increases the sugar and iron content, but eliminates the vitamin C. Dried fruit is usually served in desserts or added to cereals, etc. Extracted, concentrated juice is used as a drink. Eating apples raw ensures the maximum intake of vitamins.

Disadvantages: apple skin may upset digestion in susceptible people. There is some concern that chemical residues from sprays used in growing apples may be concentrated in the skin of the fruit. This can be overcome, to a certain extent, by peeling the fruit or eating organic.

Apricots

Description: bright orange, oval fruits about the size of a plum, with a silky skin and sweet flesh. Apricot trees originated in China, the Himalayas and temperate regions of Asia but have been grown in Europe and Britain for several centuries.

Properties: the fresh fruit is an excellent source of vitamins (especially A and C) and minerals (particularly iron and potassium). The fresh fruit is also a very good source of beta carotene, fibre and fructose. Dried apricots contain even higher amounts of beta carotene, iron, potassium and fruit sugar. Canned fruit (in natural juice) is a useful source of beta carotene, vitamin C and fibre but to a lesser extent than in other forms.

Health benefits: contain powerful, natural antioxidants – beta carotene and vitamin C. They may help to reduce the risk of heart disease, high blood pressure, certain cancers and infections. Apricots provide natural slow-release energy and useful dietary iron, which is helpful in the treatment and prevention of anaemia. Dried, 'ready to eat' apricots are considered to be excellent healthy food due to the quantity of valuable nutrients which they contain.

Cooking/serving methods: can be eaten fresh and raw but are also used in a variety of ways in desserts, cakes, stuffings, jam, etc. Apricots are used to make fruit juice and are added to many commercial foods.

Disadvantages: substances used in the drying process of apricots to preserve their bright orange colour, may provoke asthma attacks in the small number of people who are allergic to them. Apricot kernels contain prussic acid, which is poisonous.

Arrowroot

Description: the arrowroot plant is native to the West Indies, Caribbean islands and Central America. It is also grown in India, Java, the Philippines, Mauritius and West Africa. The root (rhizome) is the part used, either dried (for culinary and medicinal purposes) or fresh (as a food plant and for healing in tribal medicine).

Properties: the powdered root is a good source of starch.

Health benefits: it can be used safely to sooth an infant or build up the health of a convalescent, e.g. as a jelly or a sauce flavoured with sugar or fruit. In tribal medicine, arrowroot is used as a poultice on wounds caused by poisoned arrows or scorpion, spider and snake bites to draw out toxins. It is also used to prevent gangrene.

Cooking/serving methods: used to thicken delicate sauces.

Disadvantages: none reported.

Artichokes (globe)

Description: an unusual, oval-shaped vegetable on a stalk, that is, in fact, the flower head of the plant, and which consists of a series of stiff, overlapping leaves. The leaf bases and pinkish heart are the parts that are eaten. Globe artichokes are usually imported from Mediterranean countries.

Properties: an excellent source of vitamins, especially folate (B_9 or folic acid) minerals, (particularly potassium) and fibre.

Health benefits: contain a substance known as cynarin, along with other compounds that are believed to have healing properties. They may help to lower blood cholesterol, boost liver function and support the gall bladder in the treatment and prevention of gallstones. Artichokes and extracts containing cynarin are used in herbal medicine to treat these disorders.

Artichokes

The vegetable's content of vitamins, minerals, carbohydrate and fibre all have health-enhancing properties.

Cooking/serving methods: the tops of the leaves should be trimmed before cooking. Artichokes are usually boiled or steamed whole and the cooked leaf bases and heart are stripped off and dipped in sauce.

Disadvantages: can be 'fiddly' to eat as some parts are discarded.

Artichokes (Jerusalem)

Description: a knobbly, twisted, lumpy tuber covered by a thin, white or mauve skin concealing white flesh with a sweet flavour. They may be home grown or imported.

Properties: a good source of starch, fibre, vitamins and minerals.

Health benefits: contain vitamins, minerals and fibre essential for good health and the prevention of disease. Starch provides slow-release energy, avoiding unhelpful peaks of blood sugar.

Cooking/serving methods: usually boiled or steamed and served with butter or sauce.

Disadvantages: none known.

Asparagus

Description: a delicately flavoured vegetable consisting of the stems and flower buds, sold in small bundles. It may be home grown or imported.

Properties: a rich source of vitamins, especially A, B_9 (folic acid or folate), C and E, and minerals, beta carotene and fibre.

Health benefits: contains powerful, natural antioxidants and may help to prevent disease, including some cancers. Asparagus has known mild laxative and diuretic properties, supporting bowel and kidney functions. It is used in herbal medicine as a natural diuretic and laxative, as a sedative and to treat various other complaints such as neuritis.

Cooking/serving methods: usually gently boiled in upright bundles, leaving the buds clear of the water. May be served with butter or sauce.

Disadvantages: naturally high in substances known as purines, which can exacerbate symptoms of gout.

Aubergines (egg plant)

Description: glossy, purple-black vegetables, encircled at the base by green, papery leaves. They are roughly oval in shape and widely used in Middle Eastern, Asian and South European countries. They are originally native to India.

Properties: a useful source of vitamins, minerals and fibre.

Health benefits: contain vitamins, minerals and fibre, which are all essential for health. In African traditional medicine, the vegetables are used as a treatment for epilepsy. In Asia, they are used to relieve symptoms of measles and stomach cancer.

Cooking/serving methods: extremely versatile with distinctive texture and flavour; they are used as a basis for many dishes. Aubergines are often sliced and fried, (which greatly increases calorie content since the flesh readily absorbs oil and fat) or they can be baked, stuffed, etc.

Disadvantages: fat content is high if the aubergines are fried.

Avocado pears

Description: pear-shaped or round fruit with leathery skin and creamy, white flesh surrounding large, round stone. Their colour varies from purple-black to green, the and fruits imported from various countries including the USA (California) and the Middle East.

Properties: an excellent source of vitamins (especially B_2 (riboflavin), B_6, C and rich in E) and minerals (particularly potassium and manganese). Avocados are high in monounsaturated fatty acids and protein.

Health benefits: the vitamin content creates natural antioxidant activity, which is important in preventing disease, including some cancers. Their minerals support the health of many organs and functions, especially the nervous system. Monounsaturated fats help to lower blood cholesterol levels, which is beneficial to the heart and circulation.

Cooking/serving methods: eaten as salad vegetables, either on their own, stuffed (e.g. with prawns) or combined with other ingredients.

Disadvantages: high in calories – they may be up to 80 per cent fat or 400 calories per pear.

Balm

Description: a common garden plant in the British Isles which was naturalized into southern England at a very early period. It is also known as lemon balm, sweet balm, honey plant and cure all.

Properties: contains active ingredients that are soothing and cooling – it has a long history of use in herbal medicine.

Health benefits: may relieve feverish symptoms associated with colds and flu.

Cooking/serving methods: used as a herbal 'tea', either alone or in combination with other herbs.

Disadvantages: none reported.

Bananas

Description: familiar and popular yellow-skinned fruit

grown on plantations in many hot countries and widely exported.

Properties: contain valuable vitamins, minerals (especially potassium) and starch. They are highly digestible.

Health benefits: considered to be one of the best, natural, healthy snacks providing a ready source of energy and vitamins and minerals supportive of good health. Potassium is essential for healthy functioning of the nervous system and muscles. Palatability and digestibility make bananas an excellent weaning food for infants. They are also, good convalescent food for sick or elderly people, and are helpful in the treatment of digestive upsets and stomach ulcers.

Cooking/serving methods: eaten raw or incorporated into cakes and puddings. They are also used dried as banana chips, which concentrates the sugar content.

Disadvantages: may cause wind if eaten unripe as starch is then resistant to digestion. Rarely, they may cause allergic reactions and migraine in susceptible people. An adverse drug reaction may cause a hypertensive crisis (rapid rise in blood pressure) in susceptible people taking monoamine oxidase inhibitors (MAOIs) – a class of antidepressant drugs.

Barley

Description: a cereal grain that is a staple food in most countries of the Middle East but it is grown mainly for animal feed and for malt extract in Western countries. It is used as pearl barley (a refined form without the outer husk and much of the nutrient-rich endosperm) for culinary and medicinal purposes in Britain.

Properties: pearl barley is an excellent source of starch and it also contains a small amount of protein and fibre. Its vitamin and mineral content are low.

Health benefits: starch is a valuable source of slow-release energy, which avoids peaks of blood sugar levels. Barley water is a soothing drink used medicinally to treat children suffering from diarrhoea and sickness.

Cooking/serving methods: pearl barley is used as a nutritious 'filler' in soups and utilized commercially to make fruit-flavoured 'barley water' drinks.

Disadvantages: in common with most cereals, barley contains gluten, which must be avoided by people with coeliac disease.

Basil

Description: also known as sweet basil or garden basil, this is a herb cultivated since ancient times for culinary and medicinal use. It is a familiar garden herb in Britain and the leaves are the part used.

Properties: contains active, volatile substances that confer a distinctive flavour and aroma.

Health benefits: used in herbal medicine to treat mild nervous disorders, by acting as natural tranquillizer. It is also used to treat digestive complaints and relieve nausea.

Cooking/serving methods: used dried or fresh for flavouring, especially in tomato dishes or as herb 'tea'.

Disadvantages: none reported.

Bass (sea bass, sea wolf, sea perch, white salmon, sea dace)

Description: a round, 'white' fish with pink-tinged, delicately flavoured flesh, which is caught in the summer months.

Properties: an excellent source of protein, vitamins (particularly B_{12}) and minerals (especially iodine and iron).

Health benefits: contains protein, without fat, for repair and maintenance of tissues. It also contains vitamins and minerals that are essential for health of many body systems and functions (e.g. the nervous system and the thyroid gland).

Cooking/serving methods: usually steamed, baked or poached and served with sauce.

Disadvantages: bones may be a choking hazard; rarely, bass may cause allergy.

Bay leaves

Description: leaves from the bay laurel – an evergreen tree that grows in Mediterranean countries – are used dried or fresh as a herb and for medicinal purposes.

Properties: contain active, aromatic substances that impart a distinctive flavour.

Health benefits: may act as a tonic and stimulant to boost sluggish digestion.

Cooking/serving methods: whole, dried leaves (removed before serving), may be used to flavour stews, casseroles, etc. Shredded bay leaves form an ingredient of the mixture of herbs called *bouquet garni*.

Disadvantages: none reported.

Beans

Description: familiar vegetables that comprise a wide variety of different types and are eaten, fresh, dried or as bean sprouts. All beans contain valuable nutritional elements including protein, carbohydrate, fibre, vitamins and minerals. See individual entries.

Bean sprouts

Description: the pale, new shoots of various dried beans and peas which are usually harvested and eaten a few days after sprouting. Most types of bean or pulse can be sprouted, and the most popular are mung, aduki, chick pea, soya bean and alfalfa sprouts. Beans can be easily sprouted at home by soaking overnight in warm water and then placing them on wet cotton wool in covered containers in a warm, dark place.

Properties: an excellent source of vitamins (especially C and B vitamins) and minerals, and they provide amino acids, sugars and simple fat in readily digestible forms. They also contain carotenes.

Health benefits: provide many nutritional elements that are protective and vital for good health, and which may help to ward off diseases ranging from infections to some forms of cancer.

Cooking/serving methods: can be eaten fresh in salads, lightly stir-fried as in Chinese cookery or added at the end of cooking to soups, etc.

Disadvantages: some people suffering from lupus may be at risk of an allergic reaction to bean sprouts. Some nutritional experts believe that the health claims made for bean sprouts have been over-exaggerated.

Beef

Description: once the mainstay of the British diet, consumption of beef has steadily declined in recent years due to many adverse health scares, especially the advent of BSE, passed to humans as new variant CJD. The foot and mouth disease outbreak in 2001 has further affected beef consumption.

Properties: an excellent source of many vital nutrients, especially protein, vitamins (particularly the B group), many minerals (including iron, selenium, iodine, zinc and manganese) and other substances such as carnosine and glutathione.

Health benefits: contains many nutrients vital for health, growth and repair of body tissues, and for warding off disease. It is considered by most nutritionists to be beneficial if eaten sparingly, e.g. once a week.

Cooking/serving methods: can be roasted, grilled, fried

or used as an ingredient in stews and casseroles. Minced beef is used in numerous ways, e.g. in pasta dishes, beefburgers, sausages, etc.

Disadvantages: can be high in saturated fat, although less so than previously. Lean cuts should be selected, visible fat trimmed off and low-fat cooking methods chosen. All British beef is now considered to be safe from risk of BSE. The disease has been virtually eliminated in the UK, and animals, abattoirs and meat processing are subject to rigorous controls. Recent surveys (October, 2001) suggest that imported European beef poses a potential BSE health risk to British consumers since possibly contaminated brain and spinal cord are not always removed and controls are less strict. Other concerns centre on the chemicals, antibiotics and medicines with which cattle may have been treated. These also are subject to stringent controls and use of hormones/growth promoters is banned in European countries.

Beef 'tea' (beef stock)
Description: liquid obtained from boiling beef, traditionally used as a nutritional, convalescent food and as the basis for soups, stews and casseroles.
Properties: contains many of the nutrients present in beef.
Health benefits: contains nutrients, vitamins and minerals beneficial to and protective of health, in a readily digestible form.
Cooking/serving methods: see *Description* above.
Disadvantages: may contain saturated fat but this can be skimmed from the surface if the liquid is allowed to cool before use.

Beetroot
Description: familiar root vegetable of purple-red colour. The original wild plant is native to southern Europe

but cultivated varieties are widely distributed and can be grown in Britain. It is used as a food plant and for healing in herbal medicine.

Properties: an excellent source of fructose, vitamins (especially B9 and C), minerals (particularly potassium), carotenes, other active substances such as betacyanin (red pigment), starch and fibre.

Health benefits: contains valuable vitamins and minerals with properties essential for health. In traditional medicine beetroot is said to have anti-cancer properties and it may also act as a digestive stimulant. Although not consumed in Britain, the leaves are edible and can be eaten as a vegetable. They are a rich source of beta carotene, calcium and iron, which have known health benefits. In herbal medicine, the leaves are also used to treat various minor complaints, including toothache and headache.

Cooking/serving methods: usually boiled and cooled, and eaten as a salad vegetable or pickled in vinegar. Pickling decreases the vitamin and mineral content. Boiling until just tender enhances the mineral content and only slightly decreases the vitamin levels. The pigment may betacyanin is extracted and used commercially as a colouring agent. Sugar may also be extracted.

Disadvantages: some people are genetically unable to metabolize betacyanin, which then passes through the digestive system unchanged. If a lot of beetroot has been eaten, urine and stools my be tinged pink, which can cause alarm if mistaken for blood. The pigment is totally harmless, however.

Berries

A group of highly coloured fruits, all of which are rich sources of vitamins and natural antioxidants. They include both wild and cultivated varieties and the most familiar are bilberries, blackberries, blueberries, cranberries, loganberries, raspberries and strawberries (see individual entries). Nutritionists recommend that these fruits are eaten as frequently as possible.

Bilberries (whortleberries)

Description: small, blue-black, sweet berries that grow on low bushes in upland, moorland and wooded areas of Scotland and in Northern and Eastern Europe.

Properties: an excellent source of fructose, vitamins (especially B_9 and C), minerals, anthocyanidins and other flavonoids.

Health benefits: vitamin C and anthocyanidins have many health-enhancing effects and are natural antioxidants. Bilberries are believed to protect against many diseases and conditions, including infections and possibly, some cancers.

Cooking/serving methods: may be eaten fresh but are often stewed, with or without other fruits, and used in pies and puddings. They are also available as bottled fruit in jars.

Disadvantages: none reported.

Blackberries (brambles)

Description: large, juicy, shiny purple-black-coloured berries, borne on thorny bushes which grow wild throughout the British Isles. They are also cultivated in gardens and grown commercially. The leaves and roots are used in traditional herbal medicine.

Properties: an excellent source of fructose (fruit sugar), vitamins (especially B_9 and C) minerals, anthocyanidins and other flavonoids. A useful source of fibre.

Health benefits: fructose provides useful energy; vitamins and flavonoids have many health-enhancing effects and are natural antioxidants. Blackberries are believed to protect against many diseases and conditions, including infections and, possibly, some cancers.

Cooking/serving methods: may be eaten fresh but are often stewed and combined with apple to make fruit pies and puddings. They are also used commercially for jam making, canning, pies and puddings, and fruit juice. In herbal medicine, dried leaves are used to make 'tea' for treatment of diarrhoea, digestive upset and nasal congestion.

Disadvantages: wild, roadside berries may be polluted with pesticide or exhaust residues. Berries contain salicylate (the active ingredient of aspirin), which may cause a reaction in sensitive people.

Blackcurrants

Description: familiar, small purple-black berries with distinctive flavour and fragrance. Blackcurrant bushes are grown widely both in home gardens and in commercial cultivation. The fruit has both culinary and medicinal uses.

Properties: one of the most concentrated sources of vitamin C. Blackcurrants contain other vitamins, minerals and flavonoids, especially anthocyanidins.

Health benefits: vitamin C is vital for good health. Both vitamin C and anthocyanidins have powerful antioxidant activity. Blackcurrants have anti-infective and anti-inflammatory properties and their juice is widely used to treat sore throats. They are also used in traditional medicine in herbal 'teas' and as a remedy for fever and diarrhoea. Blackcurrants may help to protect against a variety of diseases, including some cancers.

Cooking/serving methods: may be eaten raw but usually stewed with or without other fruit for use in pies

and puddings. Blackcurrants are also used in home and commercial jam making. Commercial uses include jams, fruit juices and manufactured desserts.
Disadvantages: none reported.

Black-eyed beans
Description: one of the most popular of the pulses, black-eyed beans are smallish, buff-coloured, kidney-shaped, dried beans with a distinctive black, central mark or eye. They are grown in many countries with warm climates, especially China, southern USA and Africa, and they have a pleasant earthy flavour.
Properties: a valuable source of vegetable protein, starch and soluble and insoluble fibre. They are an excellent source of B vitamins (except B_{12}) and minerals (particularly manganese and phosphorus but also iron, magnesium and zinc).
Health benefits: can fulfil the protein needs of vegetarians when combined with cereals, grains, nuts, etc. Black-eyed beans contain vitamins and minerals that are essential for many body functions, maintenance of health, and protection against disease. Insoluble fibre promotes healthy bowel function and may protect against cancer. It also helps to lower blood cholesterol levels and is believed to protect against heart and circulatory disease. Starch provides slow-release energy, avoiding peaks of blood glucose levels, which is helpful in the prevention and control of non-insulin dependent diabetes mellitus.
Cooking/serving methods: dried black-eyed beans must be rinsed, then soaked in cold water for several hours prior to cooking. They are then boiled for about 40 mins to cook. The beans can be used in a variety of ways in stews, casseroles, curries, etc.
Disadvantages: may cause wind.

Blue cheeses

Description: full-fat cheeses with distinctive flavours, mottled with veins of greenish-blue mould. Varieties include Danish Blue, Roquefort, Stilton and Blue Cheshire.

Properties: an excellent source of protein, vitamin B_{12} and abundant in calcium, but high in saturated fat.

Health benefits: cheese provides high quality protein, especially important for vegetarians, and readily available calcium protects the health of bones. Vitamin B_{12} has many important functions and cheese provides a valuable supply.

Cooking/serving methods: usually sliced and eaten with savoury biscuits or bread but also may be used in cooked dishes.

Disadvantages: extremely high in saturated fat (about 35 per cent of total content) so should be eaten sparingly. Blue cheeses may cause allergies, e.g. eczema and migraine, in susceptible people.

Blueberries

Description: blue-black berries which grow wild on bushes in heathland and woodland but are now grown commercially. Also used medicinally in herbal medicine.

Properties: a valuable source of vitamins (especially C), minerals and anthocyanidins (flavonoids). They also provide natural fruit sugar (fructose) and fibre.

Health benefits: vitamin C and anthocyanidins are powerful antioxidants which help to protect against infection. The anthocyanidins in blueberries appear to protect against gut bacteria such as *E. coli* and are used (dried) in herbal medicine to treat digestive upsets from food poisoning and diarrhoea. In women, *E. coli* bacteria commonly stray into the urinary tract where they may cause infections such as cystitis. Eating lots of dark-coloured berries, such as blueberries and cranberries, appears to protect against recurrent cystitis. New research suggests that these berries may protect against the development of age-related eye conditions such as cataract and glaucoma.

Cooking/serving methods: can be eaten raw but usually stewed, with or without other fruit, and used in pies and puddings. Blueberries are used commercially in jams, desserts, etc.

Disadvantages: may cause allergic reaction in susceptible people.

Borlotti beans (borletti beans)

Description: one of the pulse group, borlotti beans are pinkish, speckled, kidney-shaped beans much used in Italian cookery. They are also grown in southern Europe, Africa and Taiwan, and have a mild, earthy flavour.

Properties: an excellent source of vegetable protein, fibre, starch, vitamins (especially B group) and minerals (particularly iron and manganese).

Health benefits: a useful source of protein, when combined with cereals, grains, nuts, etc., for vegetarians. Insoluble fibre in the beans promotes health of the bowel and helps to prevent constipation, diverticulitis and, possibly, cancer. Soluble fibre helps to lower blood cholesterol and may protect against heart and circulatory disease. Starch provides sustained, slow-release energy avoiding peaks of blood sugar, and is useful in prevention and control of non-insulin dependent diabetes mellitus. Vitamins and minerals have wide-ranging functions essential for health and disease prevention, including antioxidant activity.

Cooking/serving methods: must be washed and soaked

in cold water before cooking by rapid boiling for about 40 minutes. Borlotti beans can be used in stews, casseroles, pasta dishes and cold in salads.

Disadvantages: may cause wind.

Brazil nuts

Description: familiar, large, creamy-white, kidney-shaped, elongated, slightly oily nuts, encased in hard, brown shells with three edges. The trees grow in tropical/hot climates and their nuts are available either shelled or unshelled.

Properties: a good source of protein, they also contain essential fatty acids, vitamins (particularly the B group and C) and minerals (especially selenium, potassium, iron, phosphorus and copper).

Health benefits: a useful source of vegetable protein (when combined with cereals, grains, pulses, etc.) for vegetarians. Brazil nuts contain fatty acids, which are essential for health. They act as a valuable, readily accessible source of selenium and vitamin E, which have powerful antioxidant activity and are protective of health. Brazil nuts provide other minerals and vitamins essential for good health and possible prevention of disease.

Cooking/serving methods: often eaten as they are but may also be used chopped in stuffings, cakes, etc. Brazil nuts are often added to prepared muesli breakfast cereals.

Disadvantages: very high in calories due to fat content. They may trigger an allergic reaction.

Bread

Description: a staple food in most Western countries and in many other parts of the world. In Britain, there are six basic types (with many variations) along with speciality types and many imported forms. Nearly all bread is made from wheat flour but other grains, including rye and oats, may be used. All flours used for bread making in Britain have added vitamins and minerals. Most bread is raised or leavened using the activity of yeast.

Main British types of bread

White bread: made with flour from de-husked grains, hence has most of the fibre (bran) removed. May be made with bleached flour.

High-fibre white bread: made with similar flour but incorporates fibre from other sources, e.g. rice, oat bran.

Brown bread: made with flour retaining some bran content. It is usually coloured brown, e.g. with caramel.

Granary bread: made with similar flour to brown bread but incorporates malt and whole grains.

Wheatgerm bread: made with white or brown flour but incorporates a proportion of wheatgerm (from the nutritious core of the grain).

Wholemeal/wholewheat bread: made with wholemeal flour, i.e. incorporates the bran from the outer husk; or white flour with added bran and wheatgerm.

Other types of bread

Crumpet: soft, round, doughy, disc-shaped bread with honeycomb holes, served toasted.

Muffin: circular, disc-shaped, chewy roll made with wholemeal or white flour. They may be plain, savoury with cheese, or sweetened with dried fruit. They are usually toasted.

Bagel: traditional Jewish, East European, ring-shaped roll with central hole, usually made with white flour, and dipped in hot water before baking. A bagel is soft, chewy and often coated in seeds.

Bread

Brioche: light, soft, white French roll made with eggs and butter, hence it has a higher fat content than most breads.

Chapatti: Indian, unleavened flat bread, usually wholemeal.

Ciabatta: Italian, slipper-shaped loaf made with brown or white flour and olive oil, often with added herbs. It has a soft, chewy texture.

Croissant: French, light, flaky breakfast roll made with white flour and butter, hence it has a high fat content.

Naan: flat, soft, oval-shaped bread, made with white or wholemeal flour, traditionally baked in a tandoori oven and eaten with curry.

Pita: Middle Eastern and Greek, flat, oval-shaped roll made with white or wholemeal flour. It can be toasted but is usually split open to make a pocket into which a filling is inserted.

Pumpernickel: German, dark, sourish bread made with whole-ground rye flour. It has a rich, heavy texture and flavour.

Rye bread: traditional, German, Scandinavian and Russian breads made with rye flour as their main ingredient, giving a dense, dark, heavy texture and sourish flavour.

Tortilla: Mexican, unleavened, pancake-like bread made with corn and wheat flour, and baked on a griddle. Served as a base or 'wrap' for savoury fillings.

Properties: vary according to type; all British breads are an excellent source of starch, vitamins (especially B group and E), minerals (particularly calcium, iron, phosphorus, magnesium and manganese) and provide useful amounts of protein. Wholemeal, fibre-enriched loaves are an excellent source of fibre.

Health benefits: provides beneficial slow-release energy, avoiding peaks of blood sugar, which helps to prevent and control diabetes. Vitamins and minerals included in bread have many functions that are essential for health and prevention of disease. Fibre promotes healthy bowel function and helps to protect against various disorders, including cancer. Bread is considered to be a healthy food and every adult should eat at least three slices per day.

Cooking/serving methods: usually eaten plain or toasted spread with butter, margarine, jam, etc. Breadcrumbs are used in stuffings, savoury and sweet dishes. Sliced, diced bread may be used in similar ways.

Disadvantages: breads made with wheat flour contain gluten, and some people are intolerant of this, particularly those suffering from coeliac disease. There is also a relatively high salt content in most commercial breads.

Bream (sea bream, chad)

Description: broad-bodied sea fish with pinkish, delicately-flavoured flesh.

Properties: excellent source of protein, B vitamins (especially B_{12}) and useful minerals (particularly iron and iodine). It is low in fat.

Health benefits: very good source of first-class protein without accompanying fat. Contains vitamins and minerals essential for good health and for prevention of disease.

Cooking/serving methods: usually baked, poached, grilled or fried.

Disadvantages: bones can be a choking hazard; rarely bream may cause allergy.

Broad beans

Description: fairly large, fat, green, kidney-shaped beans enclosed in long, green, 'fur-lined' pods. Familiar garden vegetable in Britain and many other countries.

Properties: a good source of vegetable protein, starch, soluble fibre, vitamins (especially B_3, C and E) and minerals (including phosphorus and iron). Good source of beta carotene (carotenes) a precursor of vitamin A.

Health benefits: provide valuable vegetable protein and soluble fibre which promotes healthy bowel function and is protective against heart and circulatory disease since it helps to lower blood cholesterol levels. Broad beans contain vitamins and minerals essential to health and the prevention of disease, and beta carotene, an extremely important antioxidant.

Cooking/serving methods: young, tender beans may be boiled whole in pods. Usually, shelled beans are boiled and served as a vegetable or added to soups and stews. Skins may be tough and are sometimes removed before eating.

Disadvantages: may cause favism – an inherited disorder quite common in Mediterranean peoples – characterized by severe haemolytic anaemia (destruction of red blood cells). A person having this disorder is sensitive to the chemical vicine, which is found in the beans, because of a genetic absence of a certain enzyme involved in glucose metabolism. Some anti-malarial drugs may also trigger favism. Broad beans may also trigger a hypertensive crisis (sudden, dramatic rise in blood pressure) in susceptible people taking monoamine oxidase inhibitors (MAOIs), a class of antidepressant drugs.

Broccoli

Description: familiar garden vegetable producing dense green or purple (in purple sprouting broccoli) florets on single stalks, which unite to form a thick stem.

Properties: an excellent source of vitamins (especially C and B9) and minerals (particularly potassium and iron), beta carotene (precursor of vitamin A) and other beneficial nitrogenous substances (indoles).

Health benefits: contains vitamins, minerals, carotenes and indoles essential for good health and for protection against disease. Plant substances (phytochemicals) found in broccoli, including beta carotene and indoles, are powerful antioxidants, and are now believed to give protection against many diseases and conditions, including several cancers.

Cooking/serving methods: boiled or steamed and usually served as a side vegetable.

Disadvantages: none reported.

Brussels sprouts

Description: familiar, small, rounded cruciferous vegetables, resembling miniature cabbages, which grow in clusters upon an upright stalk. Popular winter vegetable grown throughout Britain.

Properties: excellent source of fibre, vitamins (especially C and B9), minerals (including iron), beta carotene (precursor of vitamin A) and other beneficial plant chemicals – nitrogenous indoles.

Health benefits: contain vitamins, minerals, carotenes and phytochemicals which are essential for good health and prevention of disease. Beta carotene and vitamin C have powerful antioxidant activity. Substances present in Brussels sprouts may give some protection against a number of diseases and conditions, including certain breast cancers, uterine cancer, bowel/stomach cancer and, possibly, lung cancer.

Cooking/serving methods: boiled or steamed and usually served as a side vegetable.

Disadvantages: may cause wind.

Bulgur wheat

Description: cracked wheat that is boiled and dried to form coarse granules, which are soaked before eating. Slightly chewy texture when cooked.

Properties: a good source of starch, vegetable protein, vitamins (especially the B group and E) and minerals (including iron).

Health benefits: provides slow-release energy avoiding peaking of blood sugar levels, and helpful in the prevention and control of diabetes. It is a valuable protein source for vegetarians, and contains vitamins and minerals essential for good health and prevention of disease.

Cooking/serving methods: requires soaking in boiling water for 15–20 minutes when the Bulgar wheat expands and absorbs water. It can be used as a substitute for rice in pilaf, etc.

Disadvantages: contains gluten to which some people are intolerant, and it must be avoided by people with coeliac disease.

Butter beans (Lima beans)

Description: one of the pulse group, these large, creamy-white, flattish, kidney-shaped beans are grown in Madagascar.

Properties: an excellent source of vegetable protein, starch, fibre, vitamins (especially B group) and minerals (including iron, phosphorus, magnesium, potassium and manganese).

Health benefits: provide useful protein for vegetarians. Butter beans are a source of slow-release energy, which avoids peaks of blood glucose, and are therefore helpful in the prevention and control of diabetes. Soluble fibre helps to lower blood cholesterol and reduces the risk of heart and circulatory disease. Insoluble fibre promotes healthy bowel function and may help to prevent cancer. Contain vitamins and minerals essential for many metabolic functions and are involved in the prevention of disease.

Cooking/serving methods: dried beans must be washed, soaked in cold water, rinsed then boiled in fresh water for about one and a quarter hours to cook. Cooking times vary and beans need monitoring to ensure that they do not collapse and become mushy. Canned butter beans are available but are usually high in added salt. Cooked beans are used in soups, stews, casseroles, etc.

Disadvantages: may cause wind.

Butternut squash

Description: an orange-coloured vegetable related to the pumpkin, with an outer rind surrounding succulent flesh containing large, flattish seeds. It is grown in warm climates.

Properties: good source of starch and fibre, excellent source of vitamins (especially A and E), minerals (including phosphorus, zinc, potassium, iron and magnesium) and rich in beta carotenes.

Health benefits: provides starch for slow-release energy and fibre which promotes healthy bowel function and may help to prevent cancer. Vitamin E and beta carotene are powerful antioxidants which help to protect against disease. Beta carotene is a precursor of vitamin A, which has many functions within the body, and is vital for good health.

Cooking/serving methods: may be baked, steamed, boiled and used as a vegetable or added to soups, stews, etc.

Disadvantages: none reported.

Cabbage

Description: familiar garden vegetable, of which different varieties are available all year round. Cabbage has a long history of use in traditional medicine and is grown throughout Britain.

Properties: excellent source of fibre, vitamins (especially C, K, E, B₁ and B₉), minerals (including iron and potassium) and beta carotene (carotenes). Green, leafy varieties are especially rich in nutrients.

Health benefits: contains vitamins, minerals and antioxidants that are all essential for good health and prevention of disease. Scientific research suggests that regular consumption of cabbage may help to protect against bowel cancer and oestrogen-dependent cancers in women, e.g. some breast and ovarian forms of disease. In traditional medicine, raw cabbage extract (juice) is used to encourage healing of gastric ulcers and other digestive complaints. It is believed that a chemical found in cabbage – S-methylmethionine – is responsible for this effect. Several other active substances found in cabbage are thought to be protective and are the subject of research. Dark green, outer leaves are the richest source of nutrients.

Cooking/serving methods: usually boiled and eaten as side vegetable. However, boiling causes leaching out of much of the vitamin C. Cabbage water should be saved for stocks and soups, if possible. Light steaming may preserve more nutrients. White varieties are also eaten raw in salads, coleslaw, etc.

Disadvantages: may cause wind.

Calabrese see **Broccoli**

Calamint (mountain balm, mountain mint)
Description: a bushy plant found in hedgerows and banks in Britain and Europe, the green parts of which are used in traditional herbal medicine.

Properties: contains aromatic, volatile substances believed to promote healing.

Health benefits: used in herbal medicine to treat colic, digestive complaints and wind, and also disorders of the spleen, liver and gall bladder.

Cooking/serving methods: used to make a 'tea' or syrup for medicinal use.

Disadvantages: none reported.

Cannellini beans

Description: one of the pulse group, a white form of kidney bean originating in Argentina but now widely grown, especially in Italy.

Properties: an excellent source of vegetable protein, starch, fibre, vitamins (including B group) and minerals (especially iron, magnesium, phosphorus, potassium and manganese).

Health benefits: these beans provide valuable protein for vegetarians (when combined with cereals, nuts, grains, etc.). Their starch is a source of slow-release energy, which helps to avoid peaks of blood glucose, thus assisting in the prevention and control of diabetes. Insoluble fibre promotes healthy bowel function and may help to protect against diseases of the digestive system, including cancer. Soluble fibre helps to lower blood cholesterol and reduces the risk of heart and circulatory disease. Cannellini beans contain vitamins and minerals essential for good health and prevention of disease.

Cooking/serving methods: must be washed, soaked and then cooked by vigorous boiling for up to one hour until tender. They are widely used in stews, casseroles, salads and pasta and rice dishes.

Disadvantages: may cause wind.

Cannelloni see **Wheat**

Cantaloupe melon

Cantaloupe melon
Description: a rugby-ball-shaped melon with rough, greenish-beige skin and green 'ribs'. The flesh is pleasantly scented, orange-coloured, sweet and juicy.
Properties: excellent source of vitamin C, beta carotene (vitamin A) and fruit sugar.
Health benefits: vitamin C and beta carotene are powerful antioxidants with many protective functions. Cantaloupe melon provides readily utilized energy, and the juice may act as a kidney stimulant.
Cooking/serving methods: usually eaten fresh.
Disadvantages: usually none reported.

Cape gooseberries (Chinese lanterns, physalis)
Description: small, round, golden berries surrounded by an orange-coloured, papery shell, imported from the Far East.
Properties: a good source of vitamins (especially C and A), minerals (including potassium), beta carotene (carotenes) and fructose (fruit sugar).
Health benefits: useful source of readily available energy. The Cape gooseberries contain vitamins and minerals essential for good health and prevention of disease. They also contain powerful antioxidants and have diuretic properties that may help to dissolve kidney stones.
Cooking/serving methods: may be eaten fresh but often stewed or used in preserves.
Disadvantages: none reported.

Capsicum see **Chilli peppers**

Caraway seeds
Description: aromatic seeds of the caraway plant which is a native of Europe and Asia. The seeds are used as a flavouring and in herbal medicine. An oil

derived from the plant can also be used for healing purposes.

Properties: contain volatile substances that add distinctive flavour to food and are said to promote healing.

Health benefits: used in herbal medicine to treat digestive complaints such as colic and wind, to stimulate the appetite, and for bronchitis, earache, period pains and as a poultice for bruising.

Cooking/serving methods: often used in spicy seed cake, cheeses and as a flavouring in other sweet and savoury dishes.

Disadvantages: none reported.

Cardamom seeds

Description: dried pods and seeds of the cardamom plant, a native of south-east Asia and cultivated in Sri Lanka. They are used as a spice and for healing in herbal medicine.

Properties: contain volatile, aromatic substances that add a distinctive flavour to food and are said to promote healing.

Health benefits: used in herbal medicine to treat indigestion, acid reflux, wind, colic, bad breath, headaches, coughs, colds and bronchial symptoms.

Cooking/serving methods: widely used in Indian cookery, e.g. as an ingredient of curry powder. They are also used to flavour puddings, cakes and liqueurs.

Disadvantages: none reported.

Carob

Description: pods of an evergreen tree, ground to make a powder used as a substitute for cocoa in 'chocolate' and other manufactured health foods.

Properties: a good source of carbohydrate and minerals (calcium and iron) and low in fat.

Health benefits: a source of energy and contains minerals

essential for good health. It does not contain caffeine or other stimulants.

Cooking/serving methods: usually used in manufactured foods which may or may not be low-fat alternatives to cocoa-based chocolate products, depending upon added ingredients.

Disadvantages: usually none reported.

Carrots

Description: familiar, garden root vegetable grown throughout the UK.

Properties: contain carbohydrate, fibre, vitamins and minerals but are an especially rich source of beta carotene (carotenes – vitamin A).

Health benefits: a readily accessible energy source which contains vitamins and minerals that are essential for good health and disease prevention. Beta carotene has potent antioxidant activity and may be protective against many diseases, including some cancers. Their fibre content helps to ensure healthy functioning of the bowel.

Cooking/serving methods: may be eaten raw, grated in salads, etc. They are usually, lightly boiled (which enhances uptake of beta carotene) and served as vegetable. They may also be grated as an ingredient in cakes and puddings, and diced in casseroles, stews, soups, etc. Mashed, cooked carrot is a good weaning food for infants.

Disadvantages: may contain pesticide traces – most are removed by cutting off the carrot tops and by peeling.

Catfish (rockfish)

Description: a round, bluish grey sea fish with firm, white flesh.

Properties: an excellent source of protein, vitamin B_{12} and some other vitamins and minerals (particularly iodine and iron). This fish is very low in fat.

Health benefits: supplies valuable first-class protein that is necessary for tissue growth and repair. Vitamin B$_{12}$ has vital metabolic functions including operation of the nervous system.

Cooking/serving methods: may be steamed, grilled, poached, fried, baked or mixed with other ingredients in fish dishes.

Disadvantages: fish bones can be a choking hazard. Rarely, catfish may trigger an allergic reaction.

Cauliflower

Description: popular, cruciferous garden vegetable with creamy-white, tightly packed florets forming a 'head' surrounded by green leaves.

Properties: an excellent source of vitamins (especially C), minerals, fibre and some carbohydrates. It also has sulphur-containing compounds.

Health benefits: contains vitamins and minerals essential for good health and prevention of disease and with powerful antioxidant activity. Fibre promotes healthy bowel function and may help to protect against cancer. Sulphuric compounds are also believed to protect against cancer.

Cooking/serving methods: usually boiled or steamed and served as a vegetable. It is also used in savoury dishes and sometimes raw in salads.

Disadvantages: may cause wind.

Cayenne pepper (African pepper, bird pepper)

Description: a dried, ground, brick-coloured, hot spice which is a native of Zanzibar but cultivated in most tropical and sub-tropical countries. It is used for culinary and healing purposes in herbal medicine.

Properties: contains several active, volatile substances.

Health benefits: said to be one of the purest and most effective natural stimulants in herbal medicine. It

Celeriac

produces natural warmth and is said to promote blood circulation and aid digestion. It is added to tonics and is thought to help prevent infections, especially colds and fevers. Cayenne pepper can also be used to treat chilblains.

Cooking/serving methods: added sparingly to curries, etc.

Disadvantages: 'hot' food may exacerbate certain digestive complaints.

Celeriac (celery root)

Description: the edible root of a type of celery. The brown, rough, tough, fibrous skin encloses cream-coloured flesh.

Properties: an excellent source of fibre, carbohydrate, vitamins (especially C) and minerals, (particularly potassium).

Health benefits: provides valuable slow-release energy. Soluble fibre helps to lower the level of blood cholesterol and may protect against heart and circulatory disease. Celeriac contains vitamins and minerals that are essential for good health and prevention of disease.

Cooking/serving methods: usually boiled or steamed and served as a root vegetable. Par-boiled celeriac 'matchsticks' can be fried or sautéed. Fresh, grated celeriac can be used in salads.

Disadvantages: usually none reported.

Celery

Description: familiar, succulent salad vegetable consisting of greenish white stalks and leaves with distinctive flavour. It is widely grown in Britain and is used for healing in herbal medicine.

Properties: low in calories and an excellent source of fibre and potassium. It contains several active compounds with apparent health benefits.

Health benefits: potassium plays a vital role within the body, e.g. in nerve function, balance of electrolytes and control of blood pressure. An active compound in celery (3 n-butyl phthalide) also helps to reduce blood pressure, hence it may lower the risk of a heart attack, stroke, etc. Celery contains another active compound, which is a natural anti-inflammatory, particularly helpful in relief of gout and rheumatism. In herbal medicine, celery and its seeds are used in the treatment of gout and rheumatism, and as a sedative to promote restful sleep and to relieve anxiety.

Cooking/serving methods: eaten raw in salads, stuffed with cheese filling or diced and cooked in stews, soups, etc.

Disadvantages: usually none reported.

Cereals

Description: cereal crops in one form or another are a basic, staple food for most people throughout the world. They provide starch (carbohydrate), protein, fibre, vitamins (especially B group) and minerals, the proportions varying according to type and extent to which the cereal is processed. The main cereal crops are barley, corn, millet, oats, rice, rye and wheat (see individual entries). Breakfast cereals are most commonly made from processed wheat, corn, oats or rice, sometimes in combination. All are good sources of starch, some protein, added vitamins and minerals, and some are rich in fibre. Sweetened or chocolate cereals are too high in refined sugar to be considered healthy, although they contain useful vitamins and minerals.

Chamomile 'tea'

Description: a low-growing plant with white flowers

with yellow centres and a pleasant, aromatic scent. It grows wild in the British Isles (sometimes in lawns) and Eurasia and has a long history of use in herbal medicine. In ancient Egypt, the plant was dedicated to the sun because of its extensive healing properties.

Properties: contains several active substances with wide ranging healing properties.

Health benefits: in herbal medicine, chamomile 'tea' is used for its soothing, sedative effect to relieve anxiety and nervous afflictions. It is also, used to ease indigestion, colic pains and diarrhoea. Applied externally, poultices of chamomile have antiseptic, anti-inflammatory properties and can be used to relieve minor pain, swellings, bruising, insect bites, etc. Used cold, 'tea' bags can relieve itching, inflamed eyes as may occur with hay fever and swellings of the face due to toothache or abscess.

Cooking/serving methods: as a herbal 'tea'.

Disadvantages: usually none reported.

Cheese

Description: popular food in Britain and throughout Europe, with many local and regional varieties. It is made from pressed milk curds, usually from cow's milk but sometimes from that of goats or sheep. Popular British varieties include Cheddar, Lancashire, Cheshire, Leicester, Windsor, Caerphilly and Wensleydale. Imported cheeses include Edam, Gouda, Brie, Camembert, Gruyère, Mozzarella, Ricotta, Parmesan, Feta, etc.

Properties: an excellent source of protein, minerals (particularly calcium) and vitamin B_{12} but most varieties are high in saturated fat.

Health benefits: supplies first-class protein, which is especially important for vegetarians. It is one of the best sources of calcium, helping to safeguard the health of bones and teeth. A small portion of cheese eaten at the end of a meal appears to protect teeth against decay.

Cooking/serving methods: often eaten as it is but also extensively used in cooking – in sauces, toppings, savoury baking and breads. Used commercially in a wide range of manufactured foods.

Disadvantages: should be eaten regularly but sparingly by most adults due to its high fat content. It may be a trigger for migraine.

Cherries

Description: popular, small, round, sweet, plump fruits with stones. These fruits grow on small trees, which were originally introduced into Britain in Roman times and are now widely cultivated. Cherries are valued for their healing properties in natural medicine.

Properties: a good source of fructose (fruit sugar), vitamins (especially C), minerals (particularly potassium) and flavonoids.

Health benefits: provide readily available energy, and vitamin C and flavonoids have potent antioxidant activity, helping to prevent diseases and infections. Potassium has many functions within the body. Cherries are mildly laxative and help to promote regular bowel function and relieve constipation. In traditional medicine, they are believed to contain substances that remove uric acid from blood and help to prevent gout, and cleanse and promote healthy kidney function.

Cooking/serving methods: often eaten raw, or cooked and incorporated into pies and puddings. Used commercially in desserts and as canned fruit.

Disadvantages: none usually reported.

Chervil

Description: an aromatic herb similar to parsley with aniseed flavoured leaves which grows in Europe and Asia. It is used for culinary and medicinal purposes in herbal medicine.

Properties: contains various active, volatile substances said to have healing properties.

Health benefits: used for various purposes in herbal medicine but especially as a tonic, digestive stimulant and to relieve gastrointestinal symptoms.

Cooking/serving methods: used particularly as a fresh herb to flavour soups, stews and salads.

Disadvantages: usually none reported.

Chestnuts (sweet chestnuts, Spanish chestnut)

Description: brown nuts (fruits) of the sweet chestnut tree, enclosed in outer, fleshy, prickly burr that splits when ripe. Chestnut trees grow widely in the British Isles and the nuts ripen in autumn. The leaves are used for healing in herbal medicine.

Properties: an excellent source of starch, fibre, vitamins (especially B_6 and E) and minerals. Chestnuts are low in fat and calories compared to other nuts.

Health benefits: provide helpful, slow-release energy, avoiding peaks' of blood sugar and aiding prevention and control of diabetes. They contain vitamins and minerals which are essential for good health and prevention of diseases, including those with antioxidant activity.

Cooking/serving methods: may be roasted to remove outer skin and eaten hot. Skinned nuts are also used in cooking, particularly in stuffings for poultry. Commercial uses include chestnut puree and the nuts are also added to manufactured foods.

Disadvantages: may provoke allergy.

Chicken

Description: familiar and increasingly popular form of meat used in a huge array of manufactured foods.

Properties: an excellent source of protein, vitamins (especially B group, particularly B$_3$) and minerals (especially potassium, phosphorus, zinc and iron). Vitamin and mineral proportions vary between white and dark meat. Chicken is also an excellent source of carnosine. Skinned and white meat are lowest in fat.

Health benefits: contains first-class protein, which is essential for growth and repair of tissues and organs. Vitamins and minerals are vital for health and for prevention of disease. Carnosine may play an important role in disease prevention and in protective mechanisms.

Cooking/serving methods: may be roasted, grilled, fried or boiled and is served in many different ways and incorporated into numerous dishes. Commercially, chicken is a staple ingredient of many 'ready meals' and 'fast foods'.

Disadvantages: skin has very high fat content and should preferably be removed before cooking. Chicken is a common cause of salmonella food poisoning, and raw chicken *must* be kept separate from cooked foods in the fridge, and hands should be washed before and after handling. Chopping boards and utensils used for chicken should also be thoroughly washed. Chicken *must* be properly cooked right through to ensure destruction of potentially harmful bacteria.

Chickpeas

Description: round, creamy-white 'peas' with small 'stalk', one of the most popular of the pulses. They have a slightly 'nutty' flavour and become more golden in colour when cooked. Chickpeas are widely used in Asian, Middle Eastern and Mediterranean cookery.

Properties: an excellent source of fibre, vegetable protein, starch, vitamins (especially B group and E) and minerals (particularly magnesium, iron, phosphorus, manganese and iron).

Health benefits: provide valuable protein (when combined with cereals, nuts, grains, etc.) for vegetarians. They contain insoluble fibre, which promotes regular bowel function and may protect against cancer. They also provide insoluble fibre, which helps to remove cholesterol from blood and hence may protect against heart and circulatory disease. Chickpeas provide slow-release energy, avoiding peaking of blood glucose levels, which is helpful in prevention and control of diabetes. They contain vitamins and minerals essential for many metabolic functions and which protect against disorders and disease.

Cooking/serving methods: must be washed, soaked for several hours, then rapidly boiled in fresh water for about 45 minutes to one hour. Chickpeas are usually incorporated into spicy dishes and curries but also used in vegetarian dips and spreads, particularly hummus. They are also sold tinned and ready cooked but then tend to be high in salt. They are sold commercially in manufactured vegetarian dishes.

Disadvantages: may cause wind.

Chickweed (starweed)

Description: a common small plant or weed, native to all temperate and northern regions, bearing small, white flowers shaped like stars. It can be eaten as a vegetable and is also used in herbal medicine.

Properties: a good source of vitamins (especially C),

minerals (including iron) and fibre. It is said to have anti-inflammatory properties.

Health benefits: contains vitamins and minerals essential for good health and disease prevention. Fibre promotes regular bowel function and may help in the prevention of diseases, including cancer. In traditional medicine, the dried herb is used as a herbal 'tea' to relieve rheumatic symptoms and kidney disorders. It is also used as a poultice to treat skin conditions, wounds, ulcers, bites, etc. and as an ointment for eye and skin conditions.

Cooking/serving methods: may be steamed or boiled.

Disadvantages: usually none reported.

Chicory (Belgian endive)

Description: a torpedo-shaped salad vegetable consisting of tightly packed leaves that are white with yellow-green tips. It has a distinctive, bitter taste.

Properties: contains useful vitamins (including C and B9) and minerals (iron and calcium). It is low in calories.

Health benefits: contains vitamins and minerals that are essential for good health and the prevention of disease.

Cooking/serving methods: usually eaten raw in salads but sometimes cooked as a vegetable.

Disadvantages: usually none reported.

Chicory (wild, succory)

Description: a wild herb with ragged leaves and blue flowers. The leaves can be eaten as a salad vegetable and the root is used in herbal medicine. The dried, roasted, ground root is used to make chicory 'coffee'.

Properties: an excellent source of vitamins (especially C), minerals (particularly potassium) and beta carotene.

Health benefits: contains vitamins and minerals essential

for good health and disease prevention. Beta carotene has powerful antioxidant activity. In herbal medicine, a decoction of the root is used to treat liver problems, jaundice, gout and rheumatism.

Cooking/serving methods: fresh leaves may be used in salads, and the dried, roasted ground root is used as a hot drink.

Disadvantages: usually none reported.

Chilli peppers (chillies)

Description: bright red or green fruits of the chilli plant. They are used both fresh and dried in Eastern cookery, and have a fiery 'hot' flavour, due to presence of a compound called capsaicin.

Properties: an excellent source of vitamins (especially C), minerals, flavonoids, fibre and carbohydrate.

Health benefits: contain compounds essential for maintaining good health and prevention of disease. Capsaicin makes the eyes and nose 'run', thus acting as a decongestant. Chillies may also help to lower blood pressure, 'thin' the blood and reduce cholesterol levels, all of which protect the heart and circulation.

Cooking/serving methods: diced chillies are used fresh and dried in spicy curries and Eastern dishes. Dried ground chillies are used as a powdered spice.

Disadvantages: usually eaten in too small a quantity for the vitamin, mineral and flavonoid content to contribute much to the diet. Chillies may cause irritation and exacerbate digestive complaints in susceptible people. Even handling fresh chopped chillies may cause irritation to skin and eyes.

Chives

Description: a herb related to the onion family with compact, cylindrical stalks and purple flowers. Native of temperate and northern Europe, including the British Isles, chives are used for culinary purposes and healing in herbal medicine.

Properties: contain several active compounds, minerals and vitamins.

Health benefits: an appetite stimulant, which is also said to help the digestion during recovery from illness. They may also help to prevent infections and anaemia.

Cooking/serving methods: chopped, fresh stalks and leaves are used to flavour salads, soups, stews, stuffed eggs, etc.

Disadvantages: usually none reported.

Cinnamon

Description: reddish-brown spice derived from the powdered bark of a tree that is native to Sri Lanka but which is also cultivated in other Eastern countries. It has a distinctive, aromatic flavour and is used for culinary and medicinal purposes in herbal medicine.

Properties: contains several active substances including a volatile oil.

Health benefits: in herbal medicine, cinnamon is used to treat vomiting, nausea, diarrhoea, indigestion and wind. It is also a natural nasal decongestant.

Cooking/serving methods: cinnamon 'sticks' are used to flavour punch and mulled wine. Powdered cinnamon is used in cakes and puddings, and in some savoury dishes.

Disadvantages: none usually reported.

Citrus fruits

Description: familiar fruits of trees belonging to the genus Citrus, including oranges, grapefruits, lemons, limes, satsumas, kumquats and hybrid varieties such as clementines, ortaniques and uglis. All are excellent sources of vitamin C, potassium, soluble and insoluble fibre and fructose. Eating citrus fruits and drinking their juice is one of the best ways to obtain sufficient vitamin C.

See individual entries.

Clams

Description: type of shellfish that are popular in North America but cultivated in Britain and are also available canned.

Properties: an excellent source of protein, essential fatty acids, B vitamins (especially B_{12}), minerals (particularly iron, zinc, magnesium selenium and calcium).

Health benefits: contain protein that is essential for tissue growth and repair, and fatty acids that are vital for metabolic functions and health of cell membranes. May help to lower blood cholesterol levels and protect against heart and circulatory disease. They contain vitamins and minerals which are essential for good health and disease prevention. Selenium is a powerful antioxidant with protective functions.

Cooking/serving methods: clams are sold live and should be coked and eaten on the day of purchase. Shells should be tightly closed prior to cooking – open ones should be discarded. Clams are cooked by boiling or baking until the shells open but they are sometimes sliced open and eaten raw.

Disadvantages: susceptible to pollution and like all shellfish, can be a cause of food poisoning. They are also a common trigger for allergies in susceptible people.

Clementines

Description: a popular citrus fruit that is a cross between a tangerine and an orange. They are cultivated in

Israel, Spain, Morocco, Cyprus and some Mediterranean countries.

Properties: a rich source of vitamin C, soluble and insoluble fibre, potassium and fructose.

Health benefits: vitamin C is essential for health and possesses antioxidant and anti-infective properties, which are believed to protect against a number of diseases and conditions. Insoluble fibre promotes regular bowel function and may help to protect against cancer. Soluble fibre lowers blood cholesterol levels and may protect against heart and circulatory disease. Fructose is a readily available energy source.

Cooking/serving methods: usually just eaten raw. The segments can be used to decorate desserts.

Disadvantages: usually none reported.

Cloves

Description: an aromatic spice that consists of the dried early flower buds of an evergreen tree that grows in the Far East, including the Molucca Islands and southern Philippines. They have a strong distinctive flavour. Whole cloves are used and the volatile oil derived from them. They are used in cooking and for healing in herbal medicine.

Properties: contain several active compounds in a volatile oil.

Health benefits: oil of cloves was formerly widely used to ease toothache. The oil has antiseptic and local irritant properties. In herbal medicine, cloves are given as a powder, infusion or oil to treat nausea, vomiting, wind, indigestion or as a digestive stimulant. They also act as an expectorant to relieve bronchial congestion. Clove oil is often combined with other compounds and is also widely used in commercial remedies.

Cooking/serving methods: whole cloves are used as a flavouring, especially in mulled wine, punch, etc.

Ground cloves may be combined with other spices and used to flavour cakes, puddings, etc.

Disadvantages: usually none reported.

Cockles

Description: small shellfish with circular, white, grooved shell. They are traditional seaside food.

Properties: a good source of protein, B vitamins (especially B_{12}) and rich in minerals (particularly selenium, iron and iodine). They are a useful source of helpful, essential fatty acids.

Health benefits: contain vitamins and minerals vital for good health and disease prevention including selenium (antioxidant). Cockles contain fatty acids which help to lower blood cholesterol and may protect against heart and circulatory disease.

Cooking/serving methods: usually bought ready cooked. Live cockles should be tightly shut and any open shells discarded. Cockles are cooked in boiling salted water and removed when their shells open, and served cold with vinegar or lemon juice.

Disadvantages: susceptible to pollution and a potential cause of food poisoning, if they are not eaten fresh. They are a common trigger for allergies in susceptible people.

Cocoa

Description: a powder derived from the processed, ground beans of the cacao tree which is native to tropical South America and widely cultivated, e.g. in Sri Lanka and Java. Processing produces a chocolate liquor that is used to make chocolate. Removal of most of the cocoa butter from the liquor leaves behind a solid material which is then dried and ground to produce cocoa powder.

Properties: a good source of minerals (especially iron,

potassium and magnesium). It contains mild stimulants similar to caffeine and some protein and fat.

Health benefits: a good source of useful minerals that are essential for good health. It makes a pleasant, soothing drink that can enhance feelings of relaxation. It is not overly high in calories if it is made with skimmed or semi-skimmed milk and no added sugar.

Cooking/serving methods: served as a hot drink made with milk or water. Cocoa powder is also used in home baking, and in manufactured cakes and confectionery.

Disadvantages: a common trigger for migraine and allergies.

Cod

Description: large, 'white', sea fish which is the most popular type eaten in Britain and the mainstay of traditional fish and chips. However, heavy exploitation and possibly, climate changes, threaten the survival of the species.

Properties: an excellent source of protein and vitamin B_{12} with small amounts of vitamins A and D. It contains some minerals, (including iron and iodine) and very little fat.

Health benefits: supplies valuable first-class protein necessary for tissue growth and repair. Vitamin B_{12} is involved in vital metabolic functions, including the operation of the nervous system.

Cooking/serving methods: may be steamed, grilled, poached, fried or baked and is often incorporated into a variety of fish dishes. Cod is used to produce many frozen and fresh commercial fish dishes.

Disadvantages: fish bones can be a choking hazard. Rarely, cod may be a trigger for allergy.

Cod liver oil
Description: available in supplement form as a liquid or capsules. Cod liver oil is rich in vitamins A and D, and omega-3 fatty acids which protect the heart and circulation. Cod liver oil (and that of some other fish species) may also be helpful in the treatment and prevention of arthritic complaints and skin conditions, and is a beneficial supplement for those who do not enjoy eating oily fish.

Coley (saithe, coal fish)
Description: a round sea fish, similar to cod, with white flesh when cooked.
Properties: an excellent source of protein, vitamin B_{12} and some other vitamins and minerals (especially iodine and iron). It is low in fat.
Health benefits: supplies valuable first-class protein for tissue growth and repair. It contains vitamin B_{12} which is involved in vital metabolic functions, including operation of the nervous system.
Cooking/serving methods: may be steamed, grilled, poached, fried or baked, and is used in various fish dishes.
Disadvantages: fish bones can be a choking hazard. Rarely, may trigger allergy.

Coriander
Description: pungent, aromatic herb native to southern Europe. The leaves and dried, ground seeds are used for cooking and medicinal purposes in herbal medicine.
Properties: contains volatile, active compounds, which are said to promote healing.
Health benefits: in herbal medicine, used to treat digestive complaints, such as colic and indigestion, and infections of the urinary tract.

Cooking/serving methods: powdered seeds are used as a spice, especially in Eastern cookery, to flavour curries, etc. Fresh coriander leaves can be added to soups, salads and other savoury dishes.

Disadvantages: usually none reported.

Corn (maize)

Description: a staple cereal crop grown in several parts of the world, including the Americas, Africa and Australia. The corn seeds are tightly packed together on a 'cob' or cylindrical-shaped core about 15 cm in length, and ripen to a deep golden yellow. Corn is used to produce a variety of different foods, including cornflakes (breakfast cereal), popcorn, corn meal, cornflour and corn syrup. It is also, distilled to produce bourbon (American whiskey).

Properties: provides starch, B vitamins and vitamin E, minerals (especially potassium and iron), protein and fibre. It does not contain gluten.

Health benefits: starch provides slow-release energy, avoiding peaks of blood glucose, which is helpful in the prevention and control of diabetes. B vitamins, potassium and iron play a vital part in health and disease prevention and vitamin E has known antioxidant properties. Fibre promotes regular bowel function and may help to prevent diseases, including cancer. Contains useful protein, especially when combined with other vegetable proteins. Lack of gluten makes corn a suitable cereal for those with coeliac disease.

Cooking/serving methods: corn seeds (sweetcorn) are boiled and eaten as vegetables or whole cobs may be boiled and served with melted butter. Cornflour is a fine flour used mainly in baking and as a thickening agent. Corn meal is widely used in national cuisine to make many different foods (polenta, tortillas, mealie meal). Corn syrup is used extensively commercially as a sweetening agent in manufactured foods.

Disadvantages: none usually reported.

Cottage cheese

Description: runny, white, low-fat cheese containing soft lumps, which is made from skimmed milk curds.

Properties: an excellent source of protein, calcium and vitamin B_{12}. It is low in fat.

Health benefits: contains first-class protein which is essential for tissue growth and repair, and calcium which is vital for strong bones and for possible prevention of osteoporosis.

Cooking/serving methods: usually eaten as it is, with salad, etc. Flavoured varieties (fruit and herb) are also available. Plain cottage cheese is also used in savoury and sweet dishes (e.g. low-fat cheesecake).

Disadvantages: may trigger allergy.

Courgettes (zucchini)

Description: vegetable belonging to marrow family, which has become increasingly popular in Britain and is widely grown. They have green, speckled skin and cream-coloured, firm flesh. The bright orange flowers of the plant are sometimes used in salads.

Properties: good source of fibre, vitamins (especially C and B_9) and beta carotene (carotenes).

Health benefits: fibre promotes regular bowel movement and helps to prevent diseases, including cancer. Vitamins C and B_9 are involved in vital metabolic functions and disease prevention. Beta carotene is a precursor of vitamin A and has powerful antioxidant activity. Courgettes are low in calories.

Cooking/serving methods: usually steamed, boiled, baked

or fried. They are incorporated into many savoury dishes or eaten raw in salads.

Disadvantages: usually none reported.

Couscous

Description: a wheat product made from finely ground semolina mixed with water and flour and then dried into small grains. It is the national dish in Morocco and throughout North Africa.

Properties: excellent source of starch, minerals (especially phosphorus and manganese) and some vitamins (including the B group). It is low in fat and fibre.

Health benefits: provides slow-release energy, avoiding peaking of blood sugar levels, and is therefore helpful in the prevention and control of diabetes. Couscous contains valuable minerals and vitamins that are essential for health.

Cooking/serving methods: traditionally steamed over, and served with, a spicy stew of meat and vegetables. Couscous is always cooked by steaming and can be served as alternative to rice.

Disadvantages: contains gluten so must be avoided by people with coeliac disease or wheat intolerance.

Crab

Description: familiar, shallow-sea/shoreline crustacean. Crab is a traditional British seafood.

Properties: valuable source of protein, vitamins (especially B_2, B_5 and B_6) and minerals (including zinc, potassium, magnesium and selenium). It is low in fat.

Health benefits: contains first-class protein for repair and growth of tissues. Crab provides vitamins and minerals that are vitally involved in many metabolic processes and in disease prevention, through having antioxidant activity. It may help lower blood cholesterol levels.

Crab apples

Cooking/serving methods: usually bought as 'dressed crab', i.e. ready cooked with white and dark 'meat' arranged in the shell. Live crabs are cooked by boiling. The shell is broken open and the intestine and organs are discarded. The meat is extracted from body and main claws, replaced in the shell and usually served cold with salad, bread, etc. Tinned crab (in brine) is also available. Fresh crab should be eaten within 24 hours of purchase.

Disadvantages: may provoke an allergic response, and a potential cause of food poisoning.

Crab apples

Description: small, yellow-red, sour fruits of crab apple trees which grow wild in woodlands and hedgerows of the UK. The fruits ripen in autumn.

Properties: a good source of fibre, vitamin C and minerals (especially potassium).

Health benefits: soluble fibre may lower blood cholesterol and may help to protect against heart and circulatory disease.

Cooking/serving methods: usually stewed and made into sharp-tasting jelly which is served with meats, etc.

Disadvantages: too sour to be eaten raw so they must always be cooked and require additional sugar.

Cranberries

Description: small, firm, round berries, pink to dark red in colour, which are native to North America. They have a tart, sharp taste and are used in cooking and for medicinal purposes in traditional medicine.

Properties: a rich source of vitamin C and some other vitamins and minerals. Cranberries are an excellent source of flavonoids (anthocyanidins) and fibre.

Health benefits: vitamin C and anthocyanidins have powerful antioxidant and anti-infective properties.

Cranberries have long been used in traditional North American medicine to treat urinary tract infections, and recent scientific research has isolated a compound in the berries, which appears to act against the infective bacteria. Anthocyanidins are also beneficial to the heart, circulation, joints and skin. Fibre promotes healthy bowel function and may help to lower blood cholesterol levels.

Cooking/serving methods: berries are used to make a sharp fruit sauce which is the traditional accompaniment to Christmas turkey. They may be used in other ways, but as the berries are sharp and acidic, add sugar to make them palatable. Cranberries are used commercially to produce cranberry juice.

Disadvantages: usually none reported.

Crispbreads

Description: commercially produced, baked, savoury biscuits, which are served as an alternative to bread. They are made with wheat or rye flour or a combination of both.

Properties: a good source of starch, protein, fibre, vitamins (especially B group, B_{12} and E) and minerals (particularly calcium, iron, magnesium, phosphorus, manganese and zinc) with quantities varying according to the type of flour used and production methods, etc. Crispbreads are low in fat and calories.

Health benefits: contain starch for slow-release energy, protein for tissue repair and growth and fibre for healthy bowel function. They contain vitamins and minerals that are essential for good health and prevention of disease. Crispbreads are low in calories and fat, and can be helpful for weight control.

Cooking/serving methods: used with savoury fillings or topping as a bread substitute.

Crowdie cheese

Disadvantages: like many commercial products, they may be high in salt.

Crowdie cheese

Description: traditional Scottish type of cottage cheese made from skimmed milk, but with a much finer texture. It has a pleasant, delicate flavour.

Properties: excellent source of protein, calcium and vitamin B_{12}. It is low in fat.

Health benefits: contains valuable first-class protein for tissue growth and repair, and calcium for healthy bones and teeth. Vitamin B_{12} is involved in vital metabolic functions including operation of the nervous system and production of DNA and red blood cells.

Cooking/serving methods: usually eaten with bread, crackers, etc. but may be used in cooking.

Disadvantages: may cause allergy.

Cucumber

Description: popular, greenhouse salad vegetable, native to the East Indies but cultivated in Britain since the 16th century. It is used for culinary purposes, for healing in herbal medicine and in commercial preparations.

Properties: extremely low in calories and nutrients. It has a high water content (96 per cent).

Health benefits: good, low-calorie food with mild diuretic properties. In herbal medicine, cucumber is used to cool and heal irritated skin and eyes. Cucumber extract is widely used in herbal lotions and ointments, and also in commercial products such as soaps, shampoos, skin preparations, etc.

Cooking/serving methods: almost always served as a salad vegetable but occasionally made into soup.

Disadvantages: usually none reported.

Cumin

Description: whole or ground seeds of the cumin plant, which is native to Egypt but cultivated in Eastern and Mediterranean countries. It is used as an aromatic spice and for healing in herbal medicine (although less so than formerly).

Properties: contains several compounds including a volatile oil which confers a distinctive taste. It is believed to have both stimulant and anti-spasmodic activity.

Health benefits: formerly used in herbal medicine to treat indigestion, wind and colic but now more likely to be replaced by other herbs, due to its strong flavour.

Cooking/serving methods: mainly used as whole seeds or ground spice to flavour Eastern dishes, especially curry.

Disadvantages: usually none reported.

Currants

Description: small, black, dried fruits derived from a particular variety of small, seedless grape.

Properties: high in natural sugar. A good source of fibre and minerals (especially iron and potassium).

Health benefits: provide readily available energy and fibre which promotes healthy bowel function. They contain minerals that perform essential functions within the body, including operation of the nervous system and red blood cells.

Cooking/serving methods: widely used in baking, including cakes, biscuits, buns, etc. Currants are also added to breakfast cereals and can be used as a sweetener and a healthier substitute for sweets, especially for children. Currants are widely used commercially in manufactured sweet goods.

Disadvantages: none usually reported. Should not be eaten to excess due to high sugar content.

Custard apples

Description: collective, common name for a group of exotic fruits, including the paw paw, which grow on trees in tropical climates. The fruits are heart-shaped with pulpy flesh resembling custard, contained within an outer, scaly skin. They are becoming increasingly available in British supermarkets at certain times of the year.

Properties: a good source of fruit sugar, vitamins (especially C) and minerals (including potassium). They also contain fibre.

Health benefits: provide readily accessible energy, and vitamins and minerals essential for good health and prevention of disease. They contain fibre which promotes healthy bowel function and may help to lower blood cholesterol levels.

Cooking/serving methods: usually eaten as fresh fruit or in fruit salads.

Disadvantages: usually none reported.

Dab

Description: small, flat, sea fish, which is light brown in colour with darker spots. It is sometimes available in spring.

Properties: an excellent source of protein, vitamins (especially B_{12}) and minerals (including iodine) It is low in fat.

Health benefits: provides excellent first-class protein for tissue growth and repair. Vitamin B_{12}, iodine and potassium are involved in many vital metabolic activities essential to health and prevention of disease.

Cooking/serving methods: may be poached, steamed, baked, grilled, fried or incorporated into other fish dishes.

Disadvantages: rarely may trigger allergy.

Damsons
Description: small, blue-black, dusky type of plum with red flesh and tangy flavour, borne on trees cultivated in Britain but originally native to Eurasia.

Properties: a good source of fructose, fibre, vitamins (especially C and E), minerals (particularly potassium) and flavonoids.

Health benefits: provide readily available energy and fibre, which promotes healthy bowel function, and may help to prevent diseases, including cancer. Vitamins C and E and flavonoids have anti-infective and antioxidant properties, which help to protect against a range of diseases and disorders.

Cooking/serving methods: usually stewed with sugar and used in fruit pies and puddings or in jam making. They are also used commercially for jam.

Disadvantages: usually none reported.

Dandelions
Description: familiar weed with bright yellow flowers and ragged, green leaves, growing abundantly throughout the British countryside and on waste ground. The leaves and roots can be used for culinary purposes and dandelions are widely used in herbal medicine.

Properties: the leaves are an excellent source of minerals (especially iron, potassium and calcium) and also contain beta carotene (precursor to vitamin A).

Health benefits: the leaves are a rich source of minerals involved in many metabolic functions essential that are essential for good health and disease prevention. Beta carotene has powerful antioxidant properties, helping to protect the body against disease. In herbal medicine, the leaves are used for their natural diuretic properties, and to heal digestive complaints, kidney and liver disorders and to cleanse the blood.

Dates

Dandelion is often used in combination with other herbs in natural medicines. Roasted dandelion root is ground to make a coffee substitute which may ease symptoms of dyspepsia, gout or rheumatism.

Cooking/serving methods: fresh, young leaves gathered from non-polluted areas can be used in salads (older leaves have more bitter taste). Dandelion 'coffee' is produced as a 'health' drink.

Disadvantages: usually none reported.

Dates

Description: elongated, oval, brown fruit with sweet flesh surrounding a hard, narrow stone. Fruit of the date palm has been cultivated in the Middle East and the Mediterranean since ancient times. Dates may be available fresh but more commonly as dried fruits.

Properties: rich in fruit sugar, excellent source of vitamins (especially C and B$_3$), minerals (particularly potassium but also iron, magnesium and copper) and soluble and insoluble fibre. Dried dates generally contain more concentrated nutrients (except for vitamin C).

Health benefits: readily available energy source. Dates contain useful vitamins and minerals that are essential for good health and disease prevention. Soluble fibre helps lower blood cholesterol levels and may be protective against heart and circulatory disease. Insoluble fibre promotes regular bowel function and may protect against diseases, including cancer.

Cooking/serving methods: may be eaten fresh or dried and used in baking, especially cakes. Dates are widely used in commercial manufacture of cakes and biscuits.

Disadvantages: high sugar content so should be eaten sparingly as may cause tooth decay. Dates may trigger migraine in susceptible people.

Dill

Description: herb with frond-like leaves native to the Mediterranean and south Russia but also cultivated in Britain. The aromatic leaves and dried fruits are used for culinary purposes and in herbal medicine.

Properties: contains active substances within an aromatic, volatile oil.

Health benefits: in herbal medicine, dill water is used to treat wind, indigestion and colic, and is given to babies as 'gripe water'.

Cooking/serving methods: used as a flavouring in pickles, fish dishes, soups and stews.

Disadvantages: usually none reported.

Dried fruits

Description: popular range of fruits, including raisins, sultanas, currants, apricots, peaches, figs, dates, etc. which are eaten as snacks or used in cooking. All contain valuable nutrients, the only disadvantage being that they usually have a high sugar content. See individual entries.

Dublin Bay prawns

Description: largest species of British prawn, reaching about 11 cm in length.

Properties: an excellent source of protein, vitamins (especially B_3 and B_{12}) and minerals (particularly selenium, iodine and zinc). They contain some essential fatty acids and cholesterol.

Health benefits: contain protein necessary for tissue growth and repair, and vitamins and minerals involved in many essential metabolic functions. Selenium is a potent antioxidant and essential fatty acids help to protect the heart and circulation.

Cooking/serving methods: usually sold ready-cooked

Duck

(boiled) either shelled or unshelled, and are eaten cold with salads or incorporated into savoury dishes.
Disadvantages: may trigger allergy and a potential source of food poisoning. The prawns are cooked in salted water so may be high in salt.

Duck
Description: familiar farmyard bird, reared for the table but less poplar in Britain than chicken or turkey.
Properties: excellent source of protein, B vitamins (especially B_3 and B_{12}). Duck contains double the amount of B_1 and B_2 compared to chicken). It is a rich source of minerals (especially iron – three times as much as chicken – zinc and potassium). Meat, and especially the skin, have a high fat content, mainly of the unsaturated type.
Health benefits: contains protein essential for tissue growth and repair and vitamins and minerals vital for good health and disease prevention.
Cooking/serving methods: usually roasted, raised on a trivet over a roasting pan to catch the fat, and served with vegetables and sauce.
Disadvantages: high fat content so best eaten occasionally. Most of the fat is in the skin so it is best to remove this before eating the meat.

Durum wheat
Description: the hardest type of wheat, hence it has the highest gluten content. It is used to make pasta and semolina, and is grown in the Mediterranean region. See CEREALS and WHEAT.

Eels
Description: common and familiar type of elongated freshwater fish, which migrates to the sea in order to spawn and can travel overland. They used to be

popular as jellied eels but are less so now. Eels have grey, shiny skin and white flesh.

Properties: a good source of protein, vitamins (especially B_{12}) and minerals (including iron). Contain omega-3 fatty acids.

Health benefits: contain protein essential for tissue growth and repair, and vitamins and minerals involved in vital metabolic activities and disease prevention. Eels contain fish oils that are protective of the heart and circulation and which help to prevent disease.

Cooking/serving methods: may be steamed, poached, fried, smoked or jellied.

Disadvantages: rarely, may cause allergy.

Eggs

Description: hens' eggs are a popular, inexpensive nutritious food and are widely used in home and commercial cookery. Most eggs are from intensively-reared, battery hens but eggs from free-range chickens are becoming increasingly popular and more widely available.

Properties: excellent source of protein, vitamins and minerals since designed to nourish developing chick. Eggs are high in fat (mostly unsaturated) and cholesterol.

Health benefits: contain many nutrients that are essential for good health and disease prevention. They form excellent food for both children and adults, and are especially useful for vegetarians.

Cooking/serving methods: may be boiled, poached, fried and scrambled. They are widely used in cakes, puddings, savoury dishes and manufactured foods.

Disadvantages: may trigger allergy. Some eggs contain salmonella bacteria which are a common cause of food poisoning. Salmonella is destroyed by heat so eggs should always be thoroughly cooked and dishes containing raw egg avoided. The high cholesterol content of eggs has caused concern. However, the relationship between raised blood cholesterol levels and diet is not straightforward as cholesterol is manufactured within the body. Expert advice varies between an upper limit of four to 10 eggs per week (from all dietary sources). People who have elevated blood cholesterol levels should seek medical advice on their diet.

Elderberries and elderflowers
Description: clusters of tiny, white, fragrant flowers in spring and small, purple-black berries in autumn, which are produced by the elder. This common, small tree of hedgerow and copse grows throughout Britain and Europe. The berries and flowers are used for cooking and in herbal medicine.

Properties: *flowers* have gently laxative, stimulant and astringent properties. The berries are an excellent source of fruit sugar, fibre, vitamin C and beta carotene.

Health benefits: flowers may be used to make a cordial or drink or dried for use as a 'tea'. In herbal medicine, they are used for coughs, colds, respiratory complaints and as a blood purifier. They may also be applied as paste, ointment or poultice to inflamed skin, wounds and chilblains. The berries provide energy and fibre, which promotes healthy bowel function and possible prevention of diseases, including cancer. Vitamin C and beta carotene are potent antioxidants, which help to protect against infections and diseases. In herbal medicine, the berries are used as a linctus to ease sore throats and coughs.

Cooking/serving methods: both flowers and berries are

used to make cordials and wine. The berries may also be used in fruit pies, jellies and jams.
Disadvantages: usually none reported.

Endive
Description: a salad vegetable resembling lettuce, with abundant, curly, ragged pale green-yellow leaves and a somewhat bitter flavour. Endive is popular in France.
Properties: contains some vitamins (C and B_9), minerals and beta carotene. It is low in calories.
Health benefits: provides useful nutrients that help to maintain good health and prevent disease.
Cooking/serving methods: eaten raw as a salad vegetable.
Disadvantages: usually none reported.

Fennel (Florence and garden)
Description: Florence fennel is a bulbous, white-green vegetable that consists of the swollen stem bases of the plant from which stalks and leaves arise. Garden fennel has fine, green stems and feathery leaves, and is used as a herb. Both varieties have an aniseed/liquorice flavour and produce seeds that have been used since ancient times in herbal medicine.
Properties: a good source of fibre, vitamins (especially B_9), minerals and beta carotene (precursor of vitamin A). It is low in calories.
Health benefits: contains fibre which promotes healthy bowel function and may help to prevent diseases, including cancer. Beta carotene has powerful antioxidant capabilities and helps to protect against disease. The seeds are aromatic and used to make a distillation or 'tea' to treat digestive problems, e.g. wind, bloating, colic and nausea. Fennel is used in 'gripe water' to treat infant colic and is said to promote milk flow in nursing mothers.

Fenugreek

Cooking/serving methods: Florence fennel may be served washed, chopped and raw in salads and boiled or braised and eaten as a vegetable. The leaves are used to flavour fish dishes and sauces.

Disadvantages: said to stimulate menstruation so should be avoided by pregnant women.

Fenugreek

Description: Mediterranean herb cultivated in India, Africa and Europe. The seeds are used as a flavouring and for medicinal purposes in herbal medicine. It is also used as cattle feed.

Properties: contains active compounds said to promote healing and some nutritional elements.

Health benefits: used in herbal medicine to relieve fever and stomach complaints and to help diabetes. Fenugreek is used externally as a poultice or ointment to treat skin infections. It is also used as a medicine for anaemia, gout and nervous exhaustion.

Cooking/serving methods: used as a herb for flavouring food.

Disadvantages: usually none reported.

Figs

Description: reddish-green or black fruits of the fig tree, which is native to the Middle East but widely cultivated since ancient times. They are available fresh and dried, and used for culinary purposes and in herbal medicine.

Properties: excellent source of fruit sugar, soluble and insoluble fibre, vitamins (including C) and minerals (particularly potassium, magnesium, calcium and iron). All nutrients are more concentrated in dried figs.

Health benefits: provide readily available energy, and soluble fibre, which helps to lower blood cholesterol and may help to protect against heart and circulatory disease. Insoluble fibre promotes regular bowel function and may help to prevent diseases of the digestive system, including cancer. Minerals are involved in essential metabolic functions and in the health of tissues and organs. Figs have natural laxative properties and syrup of figs is a well-known remedy for constipation. They are also used in traditional medicine to relieve catarrh, and as a poultice for mouth ulcers, tooth abscesses, boils and carbuncles.

Cooking/serving methods: eaten as fruit and also used in breads, cakes, puddings, etc.

Disadvantages: figs have a high sugar content and can cause tooth decay. They should be bought from a guaranteed source as they can be contaminated with mould toxins.

Fish

Description: comprise both 'white' and oily fish, and freshwater and marine species. All fish are excellent sources of protein, vitamins and minerals, and oily fish supply omega-3 fatty acids which are protective of the heat and circulation. See individual entries.

Flageolet beans

Description: green, kidney beans harvested while immature, and one of the pulse group of dried beans.

Properties: an excellent source of soluble and insoluble fibre, starch, vegetable protein, vitamins (especially B group) and minerals (including iron, phosphorus, magnesium, potassium and manganese).

Health benefits: soluble fibre helps to lower blood cholesterol and may protect against heart and circulatory disease. Insoluble fibre promotes regular bowel function and may protect against diseases, including cancer. Starch provides slow-release energy, which avoids peaks of blood sugar levels, and so is helpful in controlling and possibly protecting against diabetes. The beans are a valuable source of protein (when eaten with other vegetable proteins) for tissue repair and growth. They provide essential vitamins and minerals that are involved in many metabolic processes and in safeguarding health.

Cooking/serving methods: should be soaked for several hours or overnight, and then boiled in fresh water for about 45 minutes. Flageolet beans are eaten cold in salads or hot in a variety of savoury dishes.

Disadvantages: may cause wind.

Flounder

Description: brown, orange-spotted flat fish belonging to the plaice family.

Properties: an excellent source of protein, vitamins (especially B_{12}) and minerals (including iron). Low in fat.

Health benefits: provides protein that is essential for tissue growth and repair, and vitamins and minerals that are involved in vital metabolic processes, including prevention of disease.

Cooking/serving methods: may be steamed, poached, grilled or fried and eaten with accompanying vegetables or incorporated into fish dishes.

Disadvantages: rarely may trigger allergy.

French beans

Description: several varieties of green garden beans, similar to runner beans but with smaller, thinner pods.

Properties: a valuable source of soluble and insoluble fibre, vitamins (including C, A, some B vitamins, E and K), minerals (iron, magnesium and potassium) and phytochemicals (natural plant compounds).

Health benefits: provide soluble fibre which helps to

reduce levels of blood cholesterol and may protect against heart and circulatory disease. Insoluble fibre promotes regular bowel function and may protect against disease, including cancer. Vitamins and minerals are involved in vital metabolic processes and functions, including disease prevention. Phytochemicals have antioxidant and other properties that protect against diseases, including cancer.

Cooking/serving methods: usually 'topped and tailed' and boiled or steamed, whole or chopped. They are generally eaten as an accompanying vegetable.

Disadvantages: usually none reported.

Fromage frais

Description: very soft, white cheese with delicate, mild flavour.

Properties: good source of protein and excellent source of vitamins (especially B group) and minerals (particularly calcium, zinc and phosphorus). Fat content varies but many brands are low in fat.

Health benefits: provides protein that is essential for tissue growth and repair, and vitamins and minerals involved in vital metabolic functions, including protection against disease. Fromage frais is especially valuable as a source of calcium for health of bones and teeth.

Cooking/serving methods: plain fromage frais can be eaten on its own, used as a dip or incorporated into both savoury and sweet dishes. Fruit-flavoured fromage frais is a popular dessert.

Disadvantages: not suitable for those with lactose intolerance; may cause allergy.

Fruit

Description: one of the most valuable, natural, nutritious snacks or convenience foods, encompassing numerous different types from every part of the world. All fruits are valuable sources of energy, vitamins, minerals and fibre. Health experts recommend that a minimum of five portions of fruit and vegetables should be eaten each day since they are believed to protect against many diseases, including cancer. (See individual entries.) Commercially-produced fruit juices vary according to the amount of processing they have received and can have a high sugar content, although all provide valuable quantities of vitamin C. Most nutritionists agree that one glass of 'natural' (usually lower sugar) fruit juice can be counted as equivalent to one portion of fruit or vegetables.

Fulmedames beans

Description: small, spherical, dried brown beans grown in the Middle East. They are a more unusual member of the pulses group, and have a pleasant, earthy flavour.

Properties: excellent source of protein, starch, soluble and insoluble fibre, vitamins (especially B group) and minerals (including iron, potassium, manganese, phosphorus and magnesium).

Health benefits: provide valuable protein (when combined with protein from other vegetarian sources) for tissue growth and repair. Soluble fibre helps to lower blood cholesterol levels and may protect against heart and circulatory disease. Insoluble fibre promotes correct bowel function and helps to protect against diseases, including cancer. Starch provides slow-release energy, avoiding peaks of blood glucose, and is therefore helpful in prevention and control of diabetes. Vitamins and minerals perform many essential functions within the body and are involved in disease prevention.

Cooking/serving methods: beans should be rinsed and soaked in cold water for several hours, then boiled in fresh water for about one hour. They are used in stews, curries and Middle Eastern dishes.

Disadvantages: may cause wind.

Game

Description: variety of wild animals and birds that are shot and may be available at different times of the year. Species include rabbit, pheasant, duck, grouse, partridge and deer (venison).

Properties: excellent source of protein, vitamins (especially B group), minerals (including iron, potassium and phosphorus). They tend to be very low in fat and calories.

Health benefits: provides protein for tissue growth and repair, and vitamins and minerals that are essential for good health and prevention of disease. Game is free from all artificial additives.

Cooking/serving methods: may be roasted, cooked in a marinade or as an ingredient of stews and casseroles. Game needs to be hung before cooking to improve flavour and tenderness.

Disadvantages: wild birds may retain lead shot.

Garam masala

Description: a blend of spices used in eastern cookery. Composition varies but may include ground coriander, ground cumin, ground cardamom seeds and ground black pepper. These spices also have medicinal uses in traditional herbal medicine. See individual entries.

Garlic

Description: a vegetable member of the onion family, which consists of a number of segments or cloves, each surrounded by a papery skin, joined together to form a spherical bulb. Individual cloves, when peeled or crushed, have a distinctive pungent odour and are widely used to flavour savoury dishes. Garlic has been cultivated and used since ancient times for healing in traditional medicine. Scientific analysis and study of compounds contained in garlic has tended to confirm its healing benefits which are now recognized in orthodox medicine. Varieties of wild garlic are also used in herbal medicine.

Properties: contains several active substances, including sulphur compounds, which are responsible for the pungent, aromatic odour.

Health benefits: has anti-viral and anti-bacterial properties and recent studies have shown that eating raw garlic cloves reduces nasal congestion, bronchitis and cold symptoms and protects against reinfection. Compounds in garlic help to lower blood pressure and reduce levels of blood cholesterol, hence protecting the heart and circulation. It has been claimed that garlic may protect against certain cancers but there is no scientific evidence for this. Cooking may reduce garlic's health benefits.

Cooking/serving methods: may be chopped or crushed and used raw or cooked in a wide variety of savoury dishes. Garlic is used in many manufactured foods as a flavouring. Garlic oil in gelatine capsules is produced as a food supplement.

Disadvantages: makes breath smell (although taking garlic in supplement form largely overcomes this problem). Garlic may trigger migraine and handling raw cloves may cause skin rash in susceptible people.

Ginger

Description: knobbly root of a plant native to Asia but cultivated in the West Indies and Africa. It is used in cooking either as slivers of fresh root or dried and ground as a reddish-coloured spice. It has a distinctive, slightly 'hot' flavour. Ginger is also used for healing in herbal medicine.

Properties: contains several active substances and a volatile aromatic oil.

Health benefits: used to ease nausea, indigestion, wind, colic pains and diarrhoea. Ginger 'tea' helps to relieve cold symptoms and fever, and ease nasal congestion. It may boost circulation and liver function. Chewed ginger root may ease toothache.

Cooking/serving methods: fresh root is used as flavouring in spicy savoury and sweet dishes. Dried, ground ginger is usually used in desserts and baking, e.g. sponges, cakes, biscuits and puddings. Ginger is widely used commercially and also in cordials, ginger beer and ginger wine.

Disadvantages: usually none reported.

Good King Henry

Description: a herbaceous, meadow plant belonging to the goosefoot family, which grows wild in the British Isles.

Properties: a good source of soluble and insoluble fibre, vitamins (especially C and B_1) and minerals (iron and calcium).

Health benefits: provides soluble fibre which helps to lower blood cholesterol levels and may protect against heart and circulatory disease. Insoluble fibre promotes healthy bowel function and may help to protect against diseases of the digestive system, including cancer. It provides vitamins and minerals that are involved in essential metabolic functions and in maintenance of the health of tissues and organs. Vitamin C has anti-infective and antioxidant properties and is believed to protect against certain diseases and infections.

Goose

Cooking/serving methods: green leaves can be lightly boiled or steamed and eaten as a vegetable resembling spinach.
Disadvantages: usually none reported.

Goose
Description: once a popular bird for Christmas dinner but now replaced by turkey. Farmyard goose is now a rare speciality.
Properties: an excellent source of protein, vitamins (especially B group – contains twice as much B_6 and three times as much B_2 as chicken) and minerals (including iron, potassium, phosphorus). It is high in fat but most is unsaturated.
Health benefits: provides protein that is essential for tissue growth and repair, and vitamins and minerals that are involved in vital metabolic functions and the health of tissues and organs.
Cooking/serving methods: usually roasted on a trivet raised over a drip tray to allow the fat to drain. Goose is usually eaten with sauce and vegetables.
Disadvantages: high in calories so best eaten occasionally.

Gooseberries
Description: spherical, green or pinkish, slightly hairy fruits growing on thorny bushes. They are widely cultivated throughout Britain, having culinary purposes and medicinal uses in herbal medicine.
Properties: an excellent source of vitamins (especially C), minerals, soluble fibre and contain some fruit sugar. They are low in calories.
Health benefits: vitamin C has antioxidant and possible anti-infective properties, and is believed to help prevent disease as well as being involved in vital metabolic functions. Soluble fibre helps to lower blood cholesterol levels, and so may protect the heart

and circulation. Gooseberries are a source of readily available energy. In herbal medicine, they are used to treat inflammation and fever. The leaves are also used to treat 'gravel' (small kidney stones) and as a 'tonic' for adolescent girls.

Cooking/serving methods: usually not eaten raw but instead boiled with sugar for desserts, pies, crumbles or used for jam.

Disadvantages: the fruit is acidic, which may sometimes cause indigestion in susceptible people.

Grapefruit

Description: familiar, fairly large, round citrus fruits that may be yellow or pinkish red, and have a distinctive, sometimes quite sharp flavour and aroma.

Properties: an excellent source of vitamin C. Grapefruits also contain some other vitamins and minerals, soluble fibre and flavonoids (in the pith and the pulp).

Health benefits: vitamin C has important functions within the body. It is antioxidant and possibly anti-infective, helping to protect against disease. Flavonoids are also antioxidant and protective. Soluble fibre helps to lower blood cholesterol and may protect against heart and circulatory disease.

Cooking/serving methods: usually eaten fresh, cut in half, sometimes decorated with other fruits. It is also available canned and in fruit juice.

Disadvantages: usually none reported.

Grapes

Description: familiar, popular, green, black or red fruits that are grown on woody vines in Mediterranean countries and other hot climates throughout the world. Many different varieties are grown, some as dessert grapes for consumption but many more for wine making.

Green beans

Properties: high in potassium and contain other minerals and vitamins (including C) in modest amounts. They contain a useful source of fruit sugar and soluble fibre. Red and black grapes are a rich source of flavonoids.

Health benefits: potassium is an essential mineral in the body, which is involved in several functions including correct operation of the nervous system. Grapes provide readily available energy. Soluble fibre helps to lower blood cholesterol levels and may protect against heart and circulatory disease. Flavonoids are potent antioxidants and may help to prevent diseases, including cancer.

Cooking/serving methods: eaten as fresh fruit and used to decorate desserts. Particular varieties of grape are dried to produce sultanas, raisins and currants.

Disadvantages: may provoke indigestion in susceptible people. Skins can be contaminated with pesticides or bacterial or fungal moulds so grapes should be bought from a reputable source and thoroughly washed before eating.

Green beans
Description: collective name for varieties of round, green beans. See FRENCH BEANS.

Greengages
Description: a variety of small, round, green-yellow plum eaten as a dessert fruit and used in jam making. See PLUMS.

Groundnuts see **Peanuts**

Ground rice
Description: rice 'flour' mainly eaten in Britain as a sweet,

milk pudding. Nutrient content and properties are the same as those of white 'pudding' rice. See RICE.

Grouse see **Game**

Guava

Description: exotic, tropical fruit native to South America but widely cultivated in hot climates. The fruit is pear-shaped with greenish yellow skin. The flesh of the guava is sweet with an acidic 'tang' and a distinctive aromatic scent.

Properties: good source of fruit sugar, soluble fibre and very rich source of vitamin C and potassium. Guavas also contain other vitamins and minerals. One guava supplies more than the necessary daily recommended amount of vitamin C.

Health benefits: provide readily accessible energy and soluble fibre which helps to lower blood cholesterol levels and may protect against heart and circulatory disease. Vitamin C performs essential functions within the body and has antioxidant and anti-infective properties, helping to protect against disease. Potassium likewise performs vital roles within the body, including involvement in correct functioning of the nervous system.

Cooking/serving methods: usually cut in half and the flesh and seeds are scooped out and eaten fresh. The seeds are quite hard and can be discarded but their nutrient and fibre content is high so it is better to eat these too.

Disadvantages: usually none reported.

Haddock

Description: deep sea, 'white' fish, greyish in colour with dark line along its length. It has firm white flesh and is one of the most popular types of fish eaten in Britain.

Hake

Properties: an excellent source of protein, vitamins (especially B12) and minerals (including iron). It is low in fat.
Health benefits: supplies protein for tissue growth and repair, and vitamins and minerals involved in essential metabolic processes.
Cooking/serving methods: usually available as fresh or smoked fillets. Haddock may be poached, baked, steamed or fried. Haddock fillets, coated in breadcrumbs or batter, are popular convenience foods. Haddock is also used in manufactured fish dishes.
Disadvantages: rarely, may provoke allergy. If the bones are retained, they may cause a choking hazard.

Hake

Description: slender, deep sea, 'white' fish, with tender, flaky flesh.
Properties: an excellent source of protein, vitamins (especially B12) and minerals (including iron). Low in fat.
Health benefits: supplies protein for tissue growth and repair and valuable vitamins and minerals involved in essential metabolic functions.
Cooking/serving methods: best gently poached or baked.
Disadvantages: rarely, may provoke allergies.

Halibut

Description: large flatfish which sometimes reaches huge weights (up to 180 kg) but usually less. It has olive brown, marbled skin and firm, white flesh. It is only sometimes available.
Properties: an excellent source of protein, vitamins (especially B12), and minerals (including iron).
Health benefits: provides protein for tissue growth and repair, and vitamins and minerals involved in essential metabolic processes.

Cooking/serving methods: may be steamed, poached, baked or fried or used in fish dishes.
Disadvantages: rarely may provoke allergy. Bones may be a choking hazard if not removed.

Haricot beans
Description: one of the pulses group and a variety of kidney bean, but small, white and oval in shape. They are most familiar as commercially produced, canned baked beans.
Properties: excellent source of vegetable protein, soluble and insoluble fibre, starch, vitamins (especially B group) and minerals (including iron, magnesium, potassium, manganese and phosphorus).
Health benefits: provide useful protein (when combined with other vegetable proteins) for vegetarians, necessary for tissue growth and repair. Soluble fibre helps to lower blood cholesterol levels and may protect against heart and circulatory disease. Insoluble fibre promotes healthy, regular bowel function and may protect against diseases, including cancer. Starch provides slow-release energy, avoiding peaking of blood glucose levels so it is useful in the control and prevention of diabetes. Vitamins and minerals are involved in essential metabolic functions and in ensuring the health of tissues and organs.
Cooking/serving methods: must be soaked in cold water for several hours and then cooked by boiling for about an hour in fresh water. Once cooked, they can be used in wide variety of savoury dishes and salads.
Disadvantages: may cause wind.

Hazel nuts
Description: small brown nuts encased in brown shells and leafy husks, which are the fruits of hazel trees

that grow in hedgerows and copses throughout the British Isles.

Properties: a good source of protein. They are an excellent source of vitamins E and B group (especially B_1 and B_3) and minerals (including iron, phosphorus, potassium and copper). Hazel nuts are high in fat (nearly all unsaturated) and calories.

Health benefits: provide useful protein (when combined with other vegetable proteins) for vegetarians for repair and growth of tissues. They supply vitamin E, which has antioxidant properties, helping to protect against disease. Other vitamins and minerals are involved in essential metabolic processes and health of tissues and organs.

Cooking/serving methods: eaten as they are or ground. They are widely used in vegetarian dishes such as nut roast and also in cakes and desserts. In food manufacturing they are used in cakes, biscuits, confectionery, desserts and breakfast cereals.

Disadvantages: can provoke serious allergic response. May be a choking hazard and should not be given to small children.

Heart see **Offal**

Herbs
Description: a wide variety of green, leafy plants, the leaves and/or seeds of which are used for food flavouring. They are also commonly used for healing in traditional and herbal medicine. See individual entries.

Herbal 'teas'
Description: many varieties of dried herb that are available in teabags to make hot drinks with soothing and medicinal properties. Rosemary, thyme,

elderflower, nettle, peppermint, lemon balm, chamomile, dandelion and rosehip are some of the many herbal 'teas' that have become increasingly popular in Britain.

Herring
Description: small, silver, deep-sea oily fish with firm, light brown flesh. It may be sold whole and , but is also available as smoked (kippers) and pickled fish.

Properties: an excellent source of protein, vitamins (especially D and B$_{12}$), minerals (including iron, selenium) and omega-3 fatty acids.

Health benefits: provides first-class protein for tissue growth and repair and vitamins and minerals essential for good health and disease prevention. Selenium has powerful antioxidant properties. Omega-3 fatty acids in oily fish have been shown to protect the heart and circulation from disease. They are essential for the development of the eyes and brain in a growing foetus and can improve the symptoms of skin conditions such as psoriasis. Health experts recommend eating oily fish two or three times each week for its protective effect.

Cooking/serving methods: may be steamed, grilled, poached, baked or fried.

Disadvantages: salted and pickled fish have a high salt content. Pickled fish contain compounds that may trigger migraines. Herring may provoke allergy in susceptible people.

Honey
Description: honey has been prized since ancient times as a sweetener and for its medicinal properties. Although most people find honey enjoyable, soothing and beneficial, scientific evidence for many of its therapeutic effects is generally lacking.

Honeydew melon

Properties: high in simple sugars (especially glucose and
   fructose). It contains traces of minerals (calcium iron,
   phosphorus, potassium, sulphur and magnesium).
Health benefits: supplies readily accessible energy which
   can act as a tonic, e.g. in a hot drink. Honey soothes
   sore throats and cold symptoms. It has mild antiseptic
   properties and was used in traditional medicine to
   help heal wounds and burns. It is valuable as an
   alternative to sugar as it supplies some nutrients.
Cooking/serving methods: usually eaten spread on bread
   or toast and widely used as a sugar substitute and
   for flavouring in baking and sweet dishes.
Disadvantages: like all sugars, honey may cause tooth
   decay and may be unhelpful for diabetics.

Honeydew melon
Description: yellow-skinned melon in the shape of a
   rugby ball, with sweet, succulent, green to yellow-
   white flesh.
Properties: contains fruit sugar, soluble fibre, some
   vitamins (especially C) and minerals. It has a high
   fluid content and is low in calories.
Health benefits: provides useful vitamin C, which is
   essential for health, and has antioxidant properties.
   Soluble fibre helps to lower blood cholesterol levels
   and may protect against diseases of the digestive tract,
   including cancer.
Cooking/serving methods: usually eaten as it is or as an
   ingredient of fruit salad. It is sometimes used as a
   garnish.
Disadvantages: usually none reported.

Horseradish
Description: a plant cultivated in the British Isles for
   centuries. The creamy, white tap root with a coiled
   appearance has a strong, distinctive flavour and is

used to make horseradish sauce. It also has long history of use in traditional, herbal medicine.

Properties: contains several active compounds, a strong, volatile oil with antiseptic properties and some vitamins and minerals.

Health benefits: in traditional medicine, it is used as a powerful stimulant of the digestive system and to treat urinary tract infections. It is a strong diuretic and is used to treat kidney 'gravel' and stones, and cystitis, and also gout and rheumatism. A poultice of the fresh root may be applied to chilblains, facial neuralgia and rheumatic joints. Horseradish was also used (with vinegar and glycerine) to ease whooping cough and sore throats. Care must be taken when handling the root, which should be held and cut under running water. Its pungent fumes can sting the eyes and even blister the skin of sensitive people.

Cooking/serving methods: usually available as a manufactured sauce.

Disadvantages: not suitable for people suffering from thyroid problems. It should be used with caution.

Juniper berries

Description: small, round, blue-black berries of the juniper shrub, which is native to the British Isles and many other countries. Berries are used as a spice and for healing in herbal medicine.

Properties: contain several compounds within an oil obtained from the berries, which have antiseptic and diuretic properties and also act on the digestive system.

Health benefits: in herbal medicine, they are used to treat cystitis and other mild urinary tract infections, but they should not be taken if the kidneys are affected. The berries are also used for fluid retention,

Kale

    sometimes in conjunction with other diuretic herbs, and to treat wind and indigestion.

Cooking/serving methods: used as a spice, especially in some preserved foods.

Disadvantages: can cause smooth muscle to contract so should be avoided by pregnant women in case of miscarriage.

Kale (curly kale)

Description: green, or purplish, leafy vegetable with crimped, curly leaves. It is widely cultivated in Britain and elsewhere. Scientists have identified kale as being important in protecting against certain forms of cancer.

Properties: an excellent source of fibre, vitamins (especially C and B9), minerals (rich in calcium and iron), beta carotene (carotenes) and other compounds (phytochemicals), including indoles.

Health benefits: fibre promotes healthy bowel function and helps to protect against diseases of the digestive tract, including cancer. Vitamin C and beta carotene have potent antioxidant activity and are believed to protect against diseases, including some forms of cancer. Phytochemicals in kale are believed to protect against cancers of the digestive system (stomach, bowel and colon). Indoles boost liver function and help in the natural breakdown of the female hormone, oestrogen. This may be protective in some hormone-dependent cancers of the breast and female reproductive system.

Cooking/serving methods: usually steamed or boiled and eaten as a side vegetable or with sauce.

Disadvantages: may cause wind.

Kidney beans

Description: red kidney beans are one of the most familiar and popular of the pulses and are native to Central and South America, although widely cultivated in hot climates throughout the world. White and black varieties of these kidney-shaped beans are also available but are less widely used.

Properties: an excellent source of vegetable protein, starch, soluble and insoluble fibre, vitamins (especially B group) and minerals (particularly potassium, iron, zinc, magnesium and manganese). They are low in fat.

Health benefits: provide valuable protein (when combined with other vegetable proteins) for vegetarians for tissue growth and repair. Soluble fibre helps to lower blood cholesterol levels and may protect against heart and circulatory disease. Insoluble fibre promotes healthy bowel function and helps to protect against diseases of the digestive system, including cancer. Starch provides slow-release energy, helping to avoid peaks of blood glucose, which is useful in the control and prevention of diabetes. The beans supply vitamins and minerals essential for many metabolic processes, for the health of tissues and organs, and for prevention of disease.

Cooking/serving methods: dried beans should be washed, soaked overnight in cold water, rinsed, then boiled rapidly in fresh water for 15 minutes and simmered for approximately one hour. Kidney beans contain a potentially toxic substance that can cause food poisoning and this must be destroyed by rapid boiling and thorough cooking. The cooked beans are widely used in savoury cuisine throughout the world, e.g. in casseroles, salads, curries, soups, pasta and meat dishes. Canned beans (in brine) are a popular substitute for the dried variety.

Disadvantages: may cause wind. Canned beans may be high in salt and sugar.

Kidneys see **Offal**

Kiwi fruit (Chinese gooseberries)
Description: fruit of a vine native to China but adopted and made popular by growers in New Zealand. The oval, egg-sized fruits have hairy, brown skins, enclosing bright green flesh with a band of minute black seeds surrounding a slightly firmer core. The fruit is sweet, but has a sharp tangy flavour.
Properties: a good source of fruit sugar, soluble fibre, vitamins (excellent for C) and minerals (especially potassium).
Health benefits: provides readily available energy. Soluble fibre helps to lower blood cholesterol levels and may protect against heart and circulatory disease. One fruit supplies more than the daily requirement for vitamin C, which performs vital metabolic functions and has antioxidant and anti-infective properties protective against disease. Potassium has important functions within the body, including involvement in the operation of the nervous system.
Cooking/serving methods: eaten as it is or used as a garnish for sweet dishes such as cheesecake, etc.
Disadvantages: hairy skin can cause itching in people with sensitive skins.

Kohl rabi
Description: ball-shaped, green or purple vegetable, resembling a turnip, which comprises an expanded stem from which many leaf stalks arise. It is one of the vegetables of the cabbage family which experts consider may help to prevent certain forms of cancer, if eaten regularly.
Properties: a good source of soluble and insoluble fibre, vitamins (especially C), minerals (including potassium) and phytochemicals (plant compounds),

such as indoles and isothiocyanates, believed to have anti-cancer activity.

Health benefits: soluble fibre helps to lower blood cholesterol levels and may protect against heart and circulatory disease. Insoluble fibre promotes regular bowel function and helps to protect against diseases of the digestive system, including cancer. Other phytochemicals such as isothiocyanates may also help to protect against bowel cancer. Indoles promote the natural breakdown of the female hormone oestrogen, and may help to protect against some hormone-dependent cancers of the breast and reproductive system. Vitamin C is essential for the health of certain tissues and has potent anti-infective and antioxidant activity, therefore helping to protect against disease. Potassium is involved in vital metabolic functions, including the operation of the nervous system.

Cooking/serving methods: usually boiled and then used in various ways, e.g. in fritters or mashed, topped with cheese and baked.

Disadvantages: usually none reported.

Kumquats

Description: small, orange citrus fruits from China in which both skin and flesh are edible. They have a sweet, delicate flavour. They are only occasionally available.

Properties: useful source of soluble fibre, fruit sugar, vitamins (especially C) and beta carotene.

Health benefits: soluble fibre helps to lower blood cholesterol levels and may protect against heart and circulatory disease. They provide readily accessible energy. Vitamin C has anti-infective and antioxidant properties and is vitally involved in the maintenance of health of tissues and organs. Beta carotene has potent antioxidant activity, helping to protect against diseases, including some cancers.

Cooking/serving methods: usually eaten as they are or as a constituent of fruit salad. They are also used in preserves.

Disadvantages: usually none reported.

Ladies' fingers see **Okra**

Lamb

Description: traditionally one of the three meats most commonly eaten in Britain. Consumption has declined in recent years due, in part, to health concerns about eating red meat.

Properties: a rich source of protein, vitamins (especially B group) and minerals (particularly iron and zinc). Most cuts are high in saturated fat and cholesterol but lean, leg meat is comparable to other meats in fat content.

Health benefits: supplies first-class protein, essential for tissue growth and repair and vitamins and minerals involved in vital metabolic functions, health of tissues and organs and prevention of diseases.

Cooking/serving methods: may be roasted, grilled, braised, etc. or used in a variety of meat dishes, e.g. stews, casseroles, curries, etc.

Disadvantages: high saturated fat content means lamb is best eaten sparingly. High fat and cholesterol levels in the diet are linked to an increased risk of heart and circulatory disease.

Lavender

Description: purple flowers of a shrub native to the Mediterranean but widely grown as a garden plant in Britain. The flowers have a characteristic, pungent sweet scent and are widely used commercially in perfumes, air fresheners, etc. Lavender is used in herbal medicine and aromatherapy and the flowers are dried and used as 'tea'.

Properties: contains an aromatic, essential oil and various compounds said to have healing properties.

Health benefits: used in herbal medicine as a tonic for faintness, palpitations, giddiness and colic. It is also used to boost the appetite and relieve wind. Applied externally, lavender oil is used to relieve toothache, neuralgia, sprains and rheumatism. Lavender 'tea' has soothing, relaxing effects and may promote restful sleep.

Cooking/serving methods: as herbal 'tea'.

Disadvantages: usually none reported.

Leeks

Description: familiar garden vegetable belonging to the onion family, and comprising white, thick stems of tightly-packed skin layers and green leaves arising from the top, which are cut short. They are widely grown in Britain and used for healing in traditional medicine from ancient times, but less so today.

Properties: a source of fibre, vitamins (B9), minerals (especially potassium) and phytochemicals.

Health benefits: fibre promotes healthy bowel function and helps to protect against diseases of the digestive system, including cancer. Folate (B9) and potassium are involved in essential metabolic functions, health of tissues and organs, and prevention of disease. Leeks have diuretic properties and promote kidney function. They are used in traditional medicine to treat kidney stones, gout, urinary infections and also to relieve sore throats.

Cooking/serving methods: usually boiled, steamed or cooked with other vegetables in stews, casseroles, soups, etc.

Disadvantages: may cause wind.

Lemons
Description: familiar, bright yellow, citrus fruits with a sharp, sour taste. A native of India but widely cultivated in Mediterranean countries. They have many culinary uses and are also used for healing in herbal medicine.

Properties: a good source of soluble fibre, excellent source of vitamin C and contains other compounds said to have healing properties.

Health benefits: soluble fibre helps to lower blood cholesterol levels and may protect against heart and circulatory disease. Vitamin C has anti-infective and antioxidant properties, helping to protect against disease, and is involved in maintaining the health of certain tissues and organs. In herbal medicine, lemon oil is used for its tonic, cooling and astringent properties. It is used for fevers and thirst, sore throats and respiratory symptoms, hiccoughs, jaundice, palpitations and rheumatism. A lemon lotion may be applied to sunburn and sore, irritated skin.

Cooking/serving methods: widely used domestically and commercially as a flavouring and garnish, and in fruit drinks. Lemons are also used to make preserves – lemon curd, lemon cheese – and in pies and puddings.

Disadvantages: may provoke migraine in susceptible people. Lemon skins may be waxed or treated with fungicide so they should be thoroughly washed before use. The fruit is highly acidic and can cause digestive upset or tooth decay if eaten to excess.

Lemon sole
Description: brown, spotted, marine, flatfish with soft, delicate flesh with a slight lemon flavour.

Properties: an excellent source of protein, vitamins

(especially B12) and minerals (including iron). It is low in fat.

Health benefits: supplies first-class protein for tissue growth and repair, vitamins and minerals involved in vital metabolic functions and ensuring health of tissues and organs.

Cooking/serving methods: may be baked, steamed, grilled, fried, coated in breadcrumbs, etc.

Disadvantages: rarely may cause allergic response.

Lentils

Description: small members of the pulse group which come in various colours. They are widely used in Indian and Asian cuisine.

Red lentils: bright orange, split lentils which turn yellow and soft when cooked. This is the most popular and widely used type.

Brown and green lentils: small, hard lentils which maintain their shape when cooked.

Continental lentils: somewhat larger, disc-shaped, olive-green-coloured lentils with a pleasant earthy flavour.

Properties: an excellent source of vegetable protein, starch, soluble and insoluble fibre, vitamins (especially B, B6 and B9) and minerals (including iron, selenium zinc, phosphorus and manganese).

Health benefits: supply valuable protein (when combined with other vegetable proteins) for tissue growth and repair. They provide slow-release energy, avoiding peaking of blood glucose levels, and are therefore helpful in the control and prevention of diabetes. Soluble fibre helps to lower blood cholesterol levels and may help to prevent heart and circulatory disease. Insoluble fibre promotes regular bowel function and may protect against diseases of the digestive system, including cancer. Vitamins and minerals are involved in many essential metabolic functions, disease prevention and maintenance of the health of tissues and organs.

Cooking/serving methods: lentils should be rinsed in cold water but do not require soaking. They are cooked by boiling in water or in soups, stews, casseroles, curries, etc. They are an extremely versatile food used in a wide variety of ways.

Disadvantages: usually none reported.

Lettuce

Description: several varieties of salad vegetable, varying in colour from pale green to dark green to purplish-red, most of which are cultivated in Britain. Lettuce (especially the wild variety) is also used for healing in herbal medicine.

Properties: contains vitamins (C and B9), minerals (including iron) and beta carotene. Quantities vary according to type, with deeply coloured varieties usually containing more beta carotene. All varieties are very low in calories.

Health benefits: provides vitamin C and beta carotene, both of which have antioxidant effects and are believed to protect against diseases and infections. Vitamin C and B9 (folate) are involved in essential metabolic functions and in maintaining the health of certain tissues and organs. Lettuce has diuretic and mild narcotic properties, and is used in herbal medicine to treat fluid retention, coughs, colic and to induce sleep.

Cooking/serving methods: eaten fresh as salad or with bread, in sandwiches or as garnish on savoury dishes.

Disadvantages: usually none reported.

Lima beans see **Butter beans**

Limes

Description: small, green, citrus fruit with sharp, acidic, yellow flesh. The lime tree is native to Asia but cultivated in many warm climates. The fruit is widely used for food flavouring and also for healing in herbal medicine.

Properties: an excellent source of vitamins (especially C), minerals and flavonoids.

Health benefits: rich source of vitamin C, which is vitally involved in maintenance of health of certain tissues and organs and in disease prevention. In the 18th century, limes were discovered to be a cure for scurvy, and were given to British sailors on long sea voyages to prevent the disease. Vitamin C and flavonoids have important antioxidant activity, helping to protect against diseases and infections. Limes are used to ease indigestion in herbal medicine.

Cooking/serving methods: mainly used as a flavouring to enhance the flavour of other fruits or in marinades for meat. Limes are popular in Eastern cuisine in pickles, chutneys and added to curries. They are widely used commercially in food manufacturing, for flavouring, in fruit juices, etc. and also in toiletries and domestic products.

Disadvantages: none usually reported.

Liquorice (root)

Description: root of a shrub native to south-east Europe and south-west Asia and widely cultivated. It has been used as a herbal remedy in Chinese and Asian traditional medicine for thousands of years. In the West, it is also used by herbalists, and commercially, mainly in the manufacture of liquorice sweets.

Properties: contains glychrrizin (a substance which tastes sweet) along with several other compounds.

Health benefits: in herbal medicine, liquorice is a well-known remedy for respiratory complaints – coughs, bronchitis, catarrh, etc. as it is an expectorant. It is incorporated into lozenges, pastilles and cough remedies for these conditions. Liquorice has a soothing and protective effect on the stomach and digestive system and is helpful in easing the symptoms of ulcers. Chewing the root helps to protect teeth and gums from decay.

Cooking/serving methods: not applicable.

Disadvantages: should not be eaten by people with high blood pressure as liquorice can disrupt the sodium/potassium balance within the body and may exacerbate the condition.

Liver see **Offal**

Lobster

Description: large crustacean shellfish which is blue-black and brown in colour when alive but bright red-orange when cooked. It is caught in rocky, inshore waters.

Properties: an excellent source of protein, vitamins (especially B_{12} and also other B vitamins), minerals (selenium, zinc, iodine, calcium and magnesium). Lobster contains small quantities of essential fatty acids.

Health benefits: provides protein that is essential for tissue growth and repair, and vitamins and minerals involved in vital metabolic functions, health of tissues and organs, and prevention of disease. Selenium has a powerful antioxidant activity and is believed to protect against diseases including cancer. Essential fatty acids are thought to protect the heart and circulation.

Cooking/serving methods: lobster is cooked by boiling The shell and the claws are cracked open to extract the edible meat. It is often served as 'dressed lobster' with the meat arranged back in the shell. It may be eaten cold with salad, or the meat may be used in cooked dishes.

Disadvantages: may provoke allergies.

Loganberries

Description: soft fruits that are a deep purplish pink in colour, and which resemble large, seedless raspberries. They are cultivated in parts of the British Isles.

Properties: a good source of fruit sugar, soluble and insoluble fibre, vitamins (especially C), minerals (particularly potassium) and anthocyanidins (flavonoids).

Health benefits: provide readily accessible energy. Soluble fibre helps to lower blood cholesterol levels and may protect against heart and circulatory disease. Insoluble fibre promotes healthy bowel activity and may help to protect against diseases of the digestive system, including cancer. Vitamin C and anthocyanidins have powerful antioxidant and anti-infective properties and are believed to help protect the body against disease.

Cooking/serving methods: may be eaten as they are in fruit salads, etc. or cooked in fruit pies and puddings. They are also available canned.

Disadvantages: usually none reported.

Longans (dragon's eyes)

Description: small, round orange-yellow fruits of a tree native to China, related to lychees, with sweet, delicate flesh. They are only available sometimes.

Properties: a good source of fruit sugar, a rich source of vitamin C and other vitamins and minerals, including beta carotene (carotenes).

Health benefits: particularly valuable for vitamin C content. This helps to maintain the health of certain tissues and

Loquats

organs and has anti-infective and antioxidant properties. It helps to protect the body against infections and diseases, and boosts natural immunity. Beta carotene has similar important antioxidant activity.

Cooking/serving methods: usually eaten as fresh fruits or in fruit salads.

Disadvantages: none usually reported.

Loquats (Japanese plums)

Description: small, pear-shaped yellow-orange fruit with sweet, juicy flesh from a tree native to East Asia. It is only available sometimes.

Properties: a good source of fruit sugar, soluble and insoluble fibre, vitamins (but not C), minerals and beta carotene (carotenes).

Health benefits: provide readily accessible energy. Soluble fibre helps to lower blood cholesterol levels and may protect against heart and circulatory disease. Insoluble fibre promotes healthy bowel function and may protect against diseases of the digestive system, including cancer. Beta carotene has important antioxidant activity and is believed to protect against a range of diseases and conditions.

Cooking/serving methods: usually eaten or their own or in fruit salads.

Disadvantages: none usually reported.

Lovage

Description: herb native to southern Europe but with long history of cultivation in the British Isles. The aromatic seeds and stems are used for food flavouring and the leaves can be eaten in salads. The roots, leaves and seeds are used for healing in herbal medicine.

Properties: contains several active compounds and a volatile oil.

Health benefits: used in herbal medicine to treat stomach disorders, fever, urinary disorders and kidney 'gravel'. The dried leaves may be infused as a herbal 'tea'.

Cooking/serving methods: the seeds are used as a herb for food flavouring and the young leaves can be eaten as salad. The young stems can be used in a similar way to angelica, for flavouring and in confectionery.

Disadvantages: none usually reported.

Lychees

Description: fruits of a tree native to China with hard, pinkish-brown scaly skins enclosing white, succulent flesh with a central stone. The flesh is juicy and slippery with a characteristic fragrance. It is only available sometimes.

Properties: a good source of fruit sugar, vitamins (especially rich in C) and some minerals.

Health benefits: particularly valuable for vitamin C which plays an important role in the maintenance of health of certain tissues and organs. It also has anti-infective and antioxidant properties and is believed to protect against certain diseases and infections. Lychees also provide readily available energy.

Cooking/serving methods: usually eaten as fresh fruit or in fruit salad. Canned lychees are also available.

Disadvantages: none usually reported.

Macaroni see **Wheat**

Mace and nutmeg

Description: spices derived from the same plant, native to the Mollucca and Banda Islands and Malayan archipelago, and cultivated in tropical climates. Mace is the powdered, brown, lacy covering of the brown nut-like nutmeg seed. Both have a distinctive, aromatic flavour (mace is slightly stronger) and are used both for culinary purposes and in herbal medicine.

Properties: contain various active compounds and a volatile oil. One substance, myristicin, is toxic in large quantities and can cause hallucinations.

Health benefits: in herbal medicine, they are used to treat digestive complaints, wind, sickness and diarrhoea, fever, and as a tonic for the circulation.

Cooking/serving methods: used to flavour cakes, puddings, mulled wine, etc.

Disadvantages: usually none reported.

Mackerel

Description: oily sea fish with silvery blue-black, striped colouring and brownish-coloured flesh when cooked. Available fresh in season or as smoked fillets.

Properties: an excellent source of protein, vitamins (especially D and B_{12}), minerals (rich in selenium and iron) and omega-3 fatty acids.

Health benefits: provides first-class protein for tissue growth and repair, vitamins and minerals involved in maintenance of the health of tissues and organs, and in disease prevention. Selenium has powerful antioxidant activity and may protect against a number of diseases and conditions. Fish oils, such as those in mackerel, protect the heart and circulation, reducing the risk of serious conditions such as atherosclerosis and thrombosis. Health experts recommend eating oily fish two or three times each week for its protective effects. Consumption may also relieve symptoms of psoriasis and other skin conditions. Omega-3 fatty acids are needed for the development of the foetal brain and nervous system and it is recommended that women should eat oily fish during pregnancy.

Cooking/serving methods: may be baked, poached, grilled, fried and eaten with lemon juice or vegetables, etc.

Disadvantages: small bones can be a choking hazard, especially for young children and elderly people. Fresh mackerel should be cooked as soon as possible after being caught and not stored. The fish soon deteriorate and can be a source of scombroid (bacterial) food poisoning. Mackerel an provoke an allergic response in susceptible people.

Maize see **Corn**

Malt powder and extract

Description: malt powder is derived from barley grains that have been allowed to germinate, while malt extract is a syrup made from the boiled powder. The powder is used to make milk drinks and the extract is used as a sweetening agent in the food industry but is also available in jars.

Properties: an excellent source of phosphorus and magnesium. Malted milk drinks provide calcium and B vitamins (B_2 and B_{12}) as well as protein. Malt is high in natural sugar.

Health benefits: malted milk drinks, in particular, supply valuable nourishment for people who are ill or convalescing, providing energy and protein to aid recovery and essential vitamins and minerals in an easily digestible form.

Cooking/serving methods: as hot milk drinks. The syrup can be used as a sweetening agent in home baking.

Disadvantages: drinks can be made with water instead of milk for those with a milk allergy. Malt should be eaten sparingly due to high sugar content.

Mandarin oranges

Description: small, easily-peeled oranges, with sweet flesh and numerous pips, grown in Italy, Spain and Morocco. They are available fresh and also in cans.

Properties: an excellent source of vitamins (especially C but also B_1 and B_9), minerals, soluble fibre (pectin) and flavonoids.

Health benefits: provide valuable vitamin C, which is involved in essential metabolic processes and maintenance of the health of tissues and organs. Vitamin C also has anti-infective properties and helps to support the immune system. Vitamin C and flavonoids have antioxidant properties and may help to protect against disease. Soluble fibre helps to lower blood cholesterol levels and may protect against heart and circulatory disease.

Cooking/serving methods: eaten as fresh fruit or as part of fruit salad. Canned mandarins are used in same way and are popular as a topping for desserts and puddings.

Disadvantages: usually none reported.

Mangetout

Description: a variety of pea in which the pods are eaten and the peas themselves are very small.

Properties: a good source of vitamins (excellent for C), minerals (particularly potassium, beta carotene (carotenes) and fibre.

Health benefits: provide vitamin C, which is involved in essential metabolic processes and maintenance of the health of certain tissues and organs. Vitamin C and beta carotene have powerful antioxidant activity and are believed to protect against disease. Beta carotene is converted to vitamin A within the body. Potassium is involved in essential functions, including regulation of the balance between electrolytes (salts) and water in tissue fluids, and operation of the nervous system. Soluble fibre helps to lower blood cholesterol levels and may protect against heart and circulatory disease. Insoluble fibre promotes healthy bowel function and may help to prevent diseases of the digestive system, including cancer.

Cooking/serving methods: may be eaten raw in salads or lightly boiled as a vegetable.

Disadvantages: none usually reported.

Mango

Description: large, oval tropical fruit with green or orange-red skin. It has sweet, fibrous and fragrant, orange flesh and a flat, white stone.

Properties: an excellent source of fruit sugar, vitamins (rich in C), minerals, beta carotene (carotenes) and fibre.

Health benefits: provides readily available energy and essential vitamins and minerals. Vitamin C is involved in the maintenance of health of certain tissues and organs and has anti-infective properties that support the immune system. Vitamin C and beta carotene are potent antioxidants and are believed to help protect the body against certain diseases, including cancer. Beta carotene is also converted to vitamin A within the body. Soluble fibre helps to lower blood cholesterol levels and may protect against heart and circulatory disease. Insoluble fibre promotes healthy bowel function and may protect against diseases of the digestive system, including cancer.

Cooking/serving methods: usually eaten raw.

Disadvantages: none usually reported.

Marrow

Description: large, elongated vegetable, resembling giant courgette, belonging to the pumpkin family, and

cultivated in the British Isles. It has green skin dotted
with yellow, and fibrous white flesh containing edible
seeds. It is used in herbal medicine.

Properties: generally low in nutrients, comprising 95 per
cent water and small quantities of vitamins, minerals
and fibre. It is low in calories.

Health benefits: a useful vegetable for those on a calorie-
controlled diet and it contributes to the daily vitamin
and mineral intake. Marrow is used in traditional
herbal medicine as a diuretic and as a treatment for
parasitic worms.

Cooking/serving methods: may be boiled or baked (with
stuffing).

Disadvantages: usually none reported.

Melons

Description: varieties of sweet, succulent, large, fleshy
fruits including cantaloupe, charentais, galia,
honeydew and water melon.

Properties: most varieties contain vitamin C, beta
carotene (carotenes) and soluble fibre and have a
high fluid content.

Health benefits: varieties containing the highest quantities
of vitamin C and beta carotene (those with orange
flesh) are most valuable. Vitamin C is involved in
the maintenance of health of certain tissues and
organs, and has anti-infective properties which may
give some protection against viral diseases. Vitamin
C and beta carotene have powerful antioxidant
properties which may help to protect against diseases,
including cancer. Melons have natural diuretic
properties due to their high fluid content, and they
may help to boost kidney function.

Cooking/serving methods: usually served cut into slivers
or chunks as part of a fruit salad.

Disadvantages: none usually reported.

Milk

Description: almost all the milk used in the UK comes from cows, but goats' milk, which has a similar composition, is also available as an alternative. This is particularly useful for people who are allergic to cows' milk (such as some eczema sufferers), who may be able to tolerate goats' milk more readily. The only vegan alternative is soya milk, which has a different nutritional composition.

Properties: an excellent source of protein, vitamins (especially B group and vitamin A - in whole milk) and minerals (rich in calcium, zinc and phosphorus). Whole milk is high in fat. Semi-skimmed milk contains less than half the fat, while skimmed milk is almost fat-free.

Health benefits: provides protein for tissue growth and repair, and the vitamins and minerals involved in many metabolic processes and needed for healthy tissues and organs. Milk is the most important dietary source of calcium which is needed for building and maintaining strong bones and teeth. Children under the age of 5 years should not be given semi-skimmed or skimmed milk as the vitamin and calorie content is too low to meet the needs of rapid growth. Older children and teenagers should continue to drink whole or semi-skimmed milk, unless there is medical advice not to do so. Although an increasing number of children in Britain are overweight, the culprit is not milk but rather the high fat content in processed, junk foods, coupled with lack of exercise.

Cooking/serving methods: used in many different ways, e.g. in drinks, with breakfast cereals, in cooking for sauces, puddings, etc.

Disadvantages: contains lactose (a form of sugar) which some people are unable to digest. It may provoke allergies in susceptible individuals.

Millet
Description: a cereal crop cultivated in Asia and Africa where it is as a staple food.
Properties: a good source of starch, vegetable protein, vitamins (especially B group), minerals and fibre. It does not contain gluten.
Health benefits: starch provides slow-release energy, avoiding peaks of blood sugar, which is useful for control and prevention of diabetes. Millet is also a useful source of protein (especially when combined with other vegetable proteins) for repair and growth of tissues and organs. It provides vitamins and minerals that are essential for metabolic functions and health of tissues and organs. Fibre promotes regular bowel function and may help to prevent diseases, including cancer. Millet can be eaten by people with gluten intolerance.
Cooking/serving methods: can be used as an alternative to rice. Ground millet flour is made into flat breads in Asian and African cuisine.
Disadvantages: none usually reported.

Mint (see also **Peppermint**)
Description: a garden herb, widely grown in Britain. The leaves are used for food flavouring and in herbal medicine. There are several varieties, all with a highly distinctive flavour.
Properties: contains several active substances and an aromatic oil, and some vitamins and minerals.
Health benefits: mint is as a well-known digestive aid and can be used to relieve discomfort and wind. Hot mint 'tea' helps to ease cold symptoms.
Cooking/serving methods: fresh or dried mint leaves can be used to flavour a wide variety of both savoury and sweet dishes. It is also used commercially in food manufacturing and in other domestic products.
Disadvantages: none usually reported.

Mung beans

Description: small, green, round beans that belong to the pulses group. They are native to India but widely grown in warm climates. They are also familiar to us as bean sprouts..

Properties: good source of vegetable protein, starch, soluble and insoluble fibre, vitamins (especially B group) and minerals (particularly iron, magnesium, phosphorus and manganese).

Health benefits: supply complete protein (when combined with other vegetable proteins) for tissue growth and repair. They provide slow-release energy, avoiding peaks of blood glucose, and are therefore helpful in the control and possible prevention of diabetes. Soluble fibre helps to lower blood cholesterol levels and may protect against heart and circulatory disease. Insoluble fibre promotes healthy bowel function and may protect against diseases of the digestive system, including cancer. Vitamins and minerals are vitally involved in the maintenance of health of tissues and organs and in metabolic functions.

Cooking/serving methods: should be pre-soaked in cold water for several hours, then boiled in fresh water for about half an hour. Mung beans may be used in as a variety of savoury dishes, including curries, casseroles, soups and stews.

Disadvantages: may cause wind.

Mushrooms

Description: cultivated and wild varieties of edible fungi. The cultivated ones are of two main types – button or closed cup, which are small and white, and flat mushrooms, which are broader and a pale buff colour.

Properties: contain potassium and traces of other

minerals, but generally poor in nutrients. They are low in calories.

Health benefits: supply potassium, which is involved in the regulation of the balance between electrolytes (salts) and water in tissue fluids, and in nerve function.

Cooking/serving methods: may be eaten raw in salads and are often fried or cooked in stews and soups to add flavour and texture.

Disadvantages: extreme care should be taken when picking wild mushrooms to ensure that correct identification is made. Wild mushrooms can accumulate heavy metals. All fungi contain substances that may be harmful in very high doses but amounts ingested with normal consumption of mushrooms are extremely small.

Mussels

Description: bivalve (double-shelled) shellfish with inky blue-black shells that are common around British shores. They are available fresh or ready cooked and also prepared, in tins or jars.

Properties: an excellent source of protein, vitamins (especially B group, particularly B_{12}, B_2, B_9 and E), minerals (selenium, iron and iodine,) and small quantities of essential fatty acids.

Health benefits: supply protein for tissue growth and repair and vitamins and minerals that are involved in metabolic processes and essential for health. Selenium has a powerful antioxidant activity and is believed to protect against certain diseases, including cancer. Essential fatty acids in shellfish may help to protect the heart and circulation.

Cooking/serving methods: if sold live, shells should be shut. The mussels are soaked in salted water to remove grit, and then scrubbed with a brush under cold, running water. They are cooked by boiling in fresh water, when shells will open. Fresh mussels must be cooked and eaten as soon as possible after gathering. They are usually eaten as they are with bread, salad, etc.

Disadvantages: highly susceptible to contamination so they should not be gathered unless it is known that there is no pollution. Mussels are a recognized cause of food poisoning so should always be purchased from a reputable source. They are also a fairly common cause of allergy.

Mustard and cress (salad cress)

Description: salad vegetable consisting of sprouted salad rape seeds, with white stalks and tiny green leaves packed tightly together. The sprouts have a slightly hot, peppery flavour.

Properties: contains vitamins (including B_9) and minerals (such as iron). They are low in calories.

Health benefits: supply valuable vitamins and minerals involved in maintaining the health of tissues and organs and in metabolic functions.

Cooking/serving methods: served with salad and used as a garnish.

Disadvantages: usually none reported.

Mustard seeds

Description: seeds of a plant that is native to continental Europe and is also widely cultivated. Ground seeds are used as a condiment and also medicinally in herbal medicine.

Properties: contain an acrid, volatile oil with several active substances.

Health benefits: in herbal medicine, mustard seeds are used as a hot solution in a footbath, and to ease symptoms of colds and flu, headaches and neuralgia.

They are also used as a poultice to relieve acute local pain from more severe respiratory diseases such as bronchitis and pneumonia. The seeds may be used, dissolved in spirit, for chilblains and rheumatism. They have useful antiseptic properties.

Cooking/serving methods: seeds from some species of the plant are used commercially to make mustard.

Disadvantages: usually none reported.

Nectarines

Description: fruits derived and bred from peaches. They have a smooth, red and yellow skin, sweet yellow or white flesh and a central stone.

Properties: a good source of fruit sugar, fibre, vitamins (excellent for C), some minerals and flavonoids.

Health benefits: provide readily available energy. Soluble fibre helps to lower blood cholesterol levels and may protect against heart and circulatory disease. Insoluble fibre promotes regular bowel function and may help to protect against diseases of the digestive system, including cancer. Vitamins C is involved in vital metabolic functions and has anti-infective and antioxidant properties, as do flavonoids. These may help to protect against various diseases including certain cancers.

Cooking/serving methods: eaten as fresh fruit or sliced and used in desserts.

Disadvantages: usually none reported.

Nettles (stinging nettles)

Description: common weed with stinging leaves and stalks, which grows throughout the British Isles and is widely distributed elsewhere. Can be eaten as a vegetable and is used medicinally in herbal medicine.

Properties: good source of fibre, vitamins (especially C), minerals (particularly iron, potassium and calcium) and beta carotene (carotenes).

Health benefits: soluble fibre helps to lower blood cholesterol levels and may protect against heart and circulatory disease. Insoluble fibre promotes regular bowel function and may help to protect against diseases of the digestive system, including cancer. Nettles supply vitamins and minerals vitally involved in maintenance of health and disease prevention. Vitamin C and beta carotene have potent antioxidant activity and may help to protect against a number of diseases and disorders. Vitamin C has anti-infective activity and may lower the risk of contracting viral infections such as the common cold. In herbal medicine, nettle juice is used to relieve the symptoms of asthma and bronchitis. The leaves are used to treat rheumatic and arthritic complaints and to make a lotion for skin and hair conditions.

Cooking/serving methods: young leaves can be boiled or steamed in the same way as spinach.

Disadvantages: gloves must be worn and care used when picking to avoid being stung.

Nutmeg see **Mace and Nutmeg**

Nuts

Description: nuts are widely used in commercial food manufacturing and in home cooking as well as being eaten on their own. All nuts provide protein, vitamins (especially B_1, B_3 and E) and minerals (iron, potassium, phosphorus and copper). They are high in fat (but of the helpful unsaturated type) and calories and provide essential fatty acids. They can be a choking hazard and may provoke allergy. The most common types of nuts are almonds, Brazils, cashews, chestnuts, hazelnuts, pecans, pistachios and walnuts. See individual entries.

Oats

Description: cereal crop widely grown in Britain for human and animal consumption. They are mainly used in manufactured foods.

Properties: an excellent source of starch, protein, soluble fibre, vitamins (especially B group and E) and minerals. Contain gluten (a complex protein).

Health benefits: starch provides slow-release energy, avoiding peaks of blood sugar, and therefore useful in the prevention and control of diabetes. Oats supply protein, which is especially useful when combined with other vegetable proteins, for tissue growth and repair. Soluble fibre in oats lowers blood cholesterol when eaten on a regular basis and may help to protect against heart and circulatory disease. Vitamins and minerals are involved in vital metabolic processes and in maintenance of the health of tissues and organs.

Cooking/serving methods: oats are most familiar in the form of porridge oats and are also a common ingredient of breakfast cereals such as muesli. Oats and oatmeal are mainly used in home baking and desserts but also in some savoury recipes. They are widely used in commercial food manufacture – in breads, biscuits, cakes, baked goods, breakfast cereals, etc.

Disadvantages: contain gluten to which some people are intolerant.

Octopus

Description: a type of shellfish that is not widely available or popular in Britain but may be served in specialist seafood restaurants.

Properties: an excellent source of protein, vitamins (B group and especially B_3 and B_6), and minerals (rich in selenium but also includes magnesium, iodine and calcium). Octopus contains essential fatty acids.

Health benefits: provides protein for tissue growth and repair and vitamins and minerals involved in vital metabolic processes and in maintenance of the health of tissues and organs. Selenium has powerful antioxidant properties and is believed to protect against some diseases, possibly including cancer. Essential fatty acids in shellfish may help to protect against heart and circulatory diseases.

Cooking/serving methods: may be steamed, boiled, stir fried, etc. and served with salad, pasta, rice or seafood dishes.

Disadvantages: may provoke an allergic response. Octopus is prone to contamination and a potential source of food poisoning. It should be cooked and eaten as soon as possible after capture.

Offal

Description: edible, non-meat parts of animals, including organs such as the heart, liver, kidneys, brains, stomach (tripe), spleen, thymus gland (sweetbreads) and also tongue, oxtail and trotters. Since the advent of BSE, some forms of offal are now banned from the human food chain including the brain and spinal cord, spleen, intestines and thymus gland. The most popular forms of offal eaten in Britain are liver and kidney, tongue, oxtail and heart.

Properties: all are excellent sources of protein, vitamins (especially B_{12}) and minerals (particularly iron and zinc). Most are high in cholesterol. *Liver* is rich in vitamins A, B_2, B_3, B_6 and B_9. *Kidney* is a good source of vitamins B_1, B_2 and B_3. *Oxtail* is an excellent source of vitamins B2 and B6. *Heart* is an excellent source of vitamins B2 and B3.

Health benefits: provide valuable, first-class protein for tissue growth and repair and vitamins and minerals involved in vital metabolic functions, and preservation of health and disease prevention.

Cooking/serving methods: may be grilled, fried, braised or added to stews and casseroles. Tongue is usually salted and cooked by boiling.

Disadvantages: high in cholesterol so best eaten occasionally. The high level of vitamin A in liver is considered to pose a potential risk to a foetus and so it should be avoided during pregnancy. Tongue usually has a high salt content and so should be eaten sparingly.

Ogen melon

Description: round variety of melon with yellow skin crossed by pale green stripes. Its flesh is a pale, greenish yellow and it is sweet and juicy.

Properties: useful source of vitamin C. It also contains traces of other vitamins, minerals and beta carotene, and has a high fluid content.

Health benefits: provides vitamin C, which is essential for the health of blood vessels and other tissues, and with potent antioxidant and antiviral properties. It is believed to be involved in the prevention of diseases and infections. Its high fluid content may help to stimulate the kidneys. It is low in calories and hence helpful in weight control.

Cooking/serving methods: usually served as sliced fruit or as part of fruit salad.

Disadvantages: usually none reported.

Oily fish

Description: various species of freshwater and marine

fish, including salmon, trout, anchovies, herring, mackerel, sardines, tuna and pilchards (see individual entries). All are valuable sources of protein, essential omega-3 fatty acids, vitamins (B_{12} and D) and minerals (including calcium).

Okra (ladies' fingers)
Description: edible pods and seeds of a vegetable grown in hot countries, and popular in Eastern and African cuisine. Okra is available in Britain as an exotic import.

Properties: an excellent source of fibre, vitamins (including C), minerals (especially iron) and phytochemicals.

Health benefits: provides soluble fibre, which helps to lower blood cholesterol levels and may protect the heart and circulation against disease. It supplies insoluble fibre which promotes healthy bowel function and is believed to protect against digestive tract diseases, including cancer. Phytochemicals have antioxidant and other protective effects and are believed to help prevent diseases such as some cancers.

Cooking/serving methods: may be lightly boiled and served as a vegetable or added to soups, stews, casseroles, curries, etc.

Disadvantages: usually none reported.

Olives
Description: bitter black and green fruits of the olive tree, which is native to the Mediterranean and Middle East but which is widely cultivated. Olives have been prized since ancient times for their oil, which is used in cooking, and they are eaten after pickling or salting. They are also used for healing in herbal medicine.

Onions

Properties: an excellent source of vitamin E, monounsaturated fats and natural antioxidants.

Health benefits: provide fatty acids that are vital for good health. Vitamin E and natural antioxidants in olives may help to protect against diseases, including cancer. In herbal medicine, olives are used as a laxative, and are applied externally to treat sprains, bruises, rheumatism, arthritis, chills, chest and kidney complaints.

Cooking/serving methods: usually available ready processed in jars or vacuum packs. Used as a garnish on many savoury foods and the oil is extensively used for stir-frying and in salad dressings, etc.

Disadvantages: high in salt and hence not suitable for those on low sodium diets.

Onions

Description: familiar garden vegetables, originally native to south-west Asia but now cultivated in Britain and throughout the world. English onions have brown, papery skins and white, green-tinged flesh containing potent, volatile sulphur-containing compounds. They are widely used in cookery and also for healing in herbal medicine.

Properties: contain several active chemicals and substances believed to be beneficial to the heart and circulation. In herbal medicine, onions are said to have expectorant, diuretic and antiseptic properties.

Health benefits: like garlic, onions (especially when eaten raw), may help to lower blood cholesterol levels and 'thin' the blood, reducing the tendency for clots to form. Hence they may protect against heart and circulatory diseases such as atherosclerosis, thrombosis and strokes. In herbal medicine, a small roasted onion applied to the ear was used to ease earache. Onions were added to gin and the resulting fluid used to treat kidney 'gravel' and dropsy. A homeopathic remedy is made from red onions and is useful in the treatment of neuralgia, colds, hay fever, toothache and laryngitis.

Cooking/serving methods: may be eaten raw, sliced in salads, or roasted, boiled or fried and incorporated into many savoury dishes to add distinctive flavour.

Disadvantages: may trigger migraine. Onions that are eaten raw can cause bad breath and they may also cause wind.

Oranges

Description: familiar citrus fruits with tangy, sweet flesh, originally native to the Middle East but widely cultivated in warm climates. There are several different varieties available throughout the year.

Properties: an excellent source of fruit sugar, soluble fibre (pectin), vitamins (especially C, B and B$_9$), minerals and flavonoids.

Health benefits: supply readily available energy. Soluble fibre helps to lower blood cholesterol levels and may protect against heart and circulatory disease. Oranges provide vitamins and minerals that are essential for vital metabolic processes and the maintenance of health of tissues and organs. Flavonoids and vitamin C are powerful antioxidants and may help to prevent diseases, including some cancers. Vitamin C has an anti-infective activity. It may boost the immune system and help to protect against common viral infections such as colds. Essential oils are extracted from the skin and flowers of oranges and are used for healing in herbal and traditional medicine and aromatherapy.

Cooking/serving methods: usually eaten as fresh fruit but some varieties are used to make marmalade.

Disadvantages: rarely, may cause allergy.

Oregano (wild marjoram)

Description: a herb that is widely cultivated in Britain and other countries and is used to flavour food and for healing in herbal medicine.

Properties: contains a volatile oil and several active compounds said to have healing activity.

Health benefits: in herbal medicine, it is used as an infusion to treat colds and flu, measles, spasms, colic and dyspepsia. Oregano may be used externally as a poultice for rheumatic symptoms and aches and pains.

Cooking/serving methods: the herb, dried or fresh, is used to flavour savoury dishes such as pizza.

Disadvantages: may act on the uterus to promote menstruation and should not be taken in medicinal amounts during pregnancy, due to slight risk of miscarriage.

Oxtail see **Offal**

Oysters

Description: type of shellfish harvested around Britain's shores, which have been eaten for thousands of years. Prized as one of the best (and most expensive) types of shellfish and formerly believed to have aphrodisiac properties. They are also 'farmed' commercially.

Properties: an excellent source of protein, vitamins (B_{12}, B_3, B, B_2 and E) and minerals (especially zinc, copper, iodine, selenium, potassium and iron). They contain omega-3 fatty acids.

Health benefits: supply protein for tissue growth and repair, and many vitamins and minerals involved in essential metabolic functions and maintenance of the health of tissues and organs. Vitamin E and selenium have potent antioxidant activity and may help to prevent diseases, including cancer. Omega-3 fatty acids protect the heart and circulation and may help to prevent disease.

Cooking/serving methods: shells of live oysters should be tightly shut. They are cleaned and opened just before serving and may be eaten raw or lightly grilled with butter. They must be eaten absolutely fresh and are usually available only in exclusive and expensive restaurants.

Disadvantages: like all shellfish, they are a potential source of food poisoning and hence must be obtained from known, reputable source. May provoke allergy; should not be eaten in large quantities by someone who suffers from gout as they may provoke symptoms.

Papaya (pawpaw)

Description: large tropical fruit with orange-green skin. The flesh is pinky orange, sweet and succulent, and studded with numerous, brown seeds in the centre. It contains a helpful enzyme utilized in human medicine.

Properties: an excellent source of fruit sugar, fibre, vitamins (rich in C, A), minerals, beta carotene (carotenes) and an enzyme (papain).

Health benefits: provides readily accessible energy. Soluble fibre helps to lower blood cholesterol levels and may protect against heart and circulatory disease. Insoluble fibre promotes healthy bowel function and may help to protect against diseases, including cancer. Vitamin C is essential for the health of connective tissue, blood vessels and skin, etc. promotes wound healing and may boost the immune system. It has anti-infective properties and may help to protect against viral infections such as the common cold. Vitamin C and beta carotene have potent antioxidant activity and may help to protect against various diseases, including some cancers.

The enzyme papain, in papaya, is used in skin preparations for the treatment of wounds, and in pain-killing spinal injections in the USA.

Cooking/serving methods: usually eaten as fresh fruit or in fruit salads. The seeds are edible and can be dried and used as seasoning.

Disadvantages: none usually reported.

Parsley

Description: a popular garden herb, the most familiar variety having green, curly leaves. It is widely used both in cookery and also for healing in herbal medicine.

Properties: a good source of vitamins (especially C), minerals (particularly iron) and flavonoids.

Health benefits: supplies vitamins and minerals that are essential for health. Vitamin C is vital for the health of connective tissue, blood vessels, etc., promotes wound healing and may boost the immune system. It has anti-infective properties and may help to prevent common viral infections such as colds. Vitamin C and flavonoids have antioxidant activity and may help to prevent various diseases, including some cancers. In herbal medicine, a poultice of the leaves is used to soothe insect bites and stings, and other minor wounds. The root and seeds of the plant are also used to prepare medicines to treat a range of ailments.

Cooking/serving methods: may be washed and used as a garnish on salads and other savoury dishes but it is often chopped finely and used to make a sauce for fish, etc.

Disadvantages: usually none reported.

Parsnips
Description: familiar, buff-coloured root vegetable with sweet, creamy flesh and woody core.
Properties: a good source of starch, fibre, vitamins (especially C, E and B9) and some minerals.
Health benefits: supply starch for slow-release energy, avoiding peaking of blood glucose levels, and hence useful in the control and possible prevention of diabetes. Fibre promotes healthy bowel function and may help to prevent diseases of the digestive system, including cancer. Vitamin C is necessary for the health of connective tissue and blood vessels. promotes wound healing and may boost the immune system. It may also help to protect against viral infections such as the common cold. Vitamins C and E are powerful antioxidants and may help to prevent diseases, including cancer.
Cooking/serving methods: roasted, boiled, baked, eaten as a vegetable or incorporated into various savoury dishes.
Disadvantages: usually none reported.

Partridge see **Game**

Passion fruits
Description: exotic, tropical fruits native to Brazil with purple, wrinkled skin and highly fragrant, sweet, orange flesh interspersed with numerous black seeds.
Properties: a good source of fruit sugar, fibre, vitamins (especially C) and minerals (including potassium).
Health benefits: provide readily available energy. Soluble fibre helps to lower blood cholesterol levels, possibly reducing the risk of heart and circulatory disease. Insoluble fibre promotes regular bowel function and may help to prevent diseases of the digestive system, including cancer. Vitamin C is vital for the health of

tissues such as blood vessels and may boost the immune system. It also has anti-infective properties that may help to prevent common viral infections such as colds. Potassium performs many vital functions including regulation of electrolyte (salts) levels in tissue fluids and operation of nerves.

Cooking/serving methods: eaten as fresh fruits or as part of fruit salads.

Disadvantages: usually none reported.

Pasta see **Wheat**

Peaches

Description: popular fruits imported from Mediterranean countries and California, with soft, downy, pinky yellow skin and sweet, succulent golden flesh surrounding a large central stone.

Properties: a good source of fruit sugar, fibre, vitamins (especially C) and beta carotene (carotenes). They are easily digested and mildly laxative.

Health benefits: supply readily accessible energy. Soluble fibre helps to lower blood cholesterol levels and may protect against heart and circulatory disease. Insoluble fibre promotes regularity of bowel function and may help to prevent diseases of the digestive system, including cancer. Vitamin C is essential for the health of connective tissues and blood vessels. It promotes wound healing and may boost the immune system. It has anti-infective properties and may help to protect against common viral diseases such as colds. Vitamin C and beta carotene have antioxidant activity which may help to protect against a range of diseases, including cancer.

Cooking/serving methods: usually eaten as raw fruit but sometimes baked or incorporated into desserts. Peaches are available as commercially-prepared canned fruit (in which most of vitamin C is lost) and also dried.

Disadvantages: usually none reported.

Peanuts (ground nuts)

Description: one of the most popular forms of nuts. Peanuts are, in fact, legumes like peas and beans, as distinct from true nuts which grow on trees. The dry, crinkly, buff-coloured shells correspond to the pods of peas and beans and enclose several creamy nuts, encased in brown, papery skins. Peanuts are available with or without their shells but are most popular as salted nuts. They are used commercially to make peanut butter and are included in a wide variety of manufactured foods.

Properties: an excellent source of protein, vitamins (especially B group and E), minerals (including potassium iron, copper and phosphorus). Peanuts are high in unsaturated fats and essential fatty acids.

Health benefits: provide valuable nutrients, especially for vegans and vegetarians, supplying some of the vitamins, minerals and fatty acids more readily obtained from animal sources. Peanuts supply protein (this becomes complete when combined with protein from other vegetable sources) for tissue growth and repair, and vitamins and minerals that are essential for good health. Vitamin E has powerful antioxidant activity and may help to protect against diseases, including cancer.

Cooking/serving methods: usually eaten as plain or roasted, salted nuts.

Disadvantages: can provoke severe or fatal allergy. They are also a choking hazard and should not be given to small children. Peanuts are high in calories and subject to contamination with moulds that can produce dangerous poisons (aflatoxins) so they *must* be bought from a reputable source. Peanuts that are bought for wild birds should not be eaten by people.

Pearl barley see **Barley**

Pears

Description: popular fruits of many different varieties, several of which are grown in Britain. Familiar types include Conference, William and Comice.

Properties: an excellent source of fruit sugar, soluble fibre, vitamins (especially C) and minerals (particularly potassium). They are readily digestible.

Health benefits: provide readily available energy. Soluble fibre helps to lower blood cholesterol levels and may protect against heart and circulatory disease. Vitamin C has antioxidant and anti-infective activity and is essential for the health of connective tissues, blood vessels, etc. It promotes wound healing, may boost the immune system and may also give some protection against viral infections such as the common cold and some other diseases.

Cooking/serving methods: often eaten as fresh fruit but may be gently stewed or baked or incorporated into desserts. Pears are commercially available as tinned and dried fruit.

Disadvantages: usually none reported.

Peas (fresh garden peas)

Description: familiar and popular garden vegetables grown throughout the British Isles and commercially available as ready-shelled frozen peas and as canned vegetables.

Properties: a good source of vegetable sugar, starch and protein. Excellent source of fibre, vitamins (particularly C, B_1 and B_9), minerals (especially phosphorus) and phytochemicals.

Health benefits: supply readily available energy and some protein needed for repair and growth of tissues and organs. Peas provide soluble fibre which helps to lower blood cholesterol levels and may protect the heart and circulation against disease. They contain insoluble fibre which promotes healthy bowel function and may protect against diseases of the digestive tract, including cancer. They also provide vitamins and minerals that are essential for metabolic functions, the maintenance of health and prevention of disease. Vitamin C and phytochemicals have antioxidant properties and vitamin C has anti-infective activity, helping to protect against diseases and infections.

Cooking/serving methods: usually lightly boiled (after shelling) and served as a vegetable or incorporated into a wide variety of savoury dishes and salads. Commercially, frozen peas are a good substitute for fresh, garden peas although they lose some of their vitamin content during processing. Canned peas may be high in salt and sugar and lose most of their vitamin C during processing.

Disadvantages: usually none reported.

Peas (dried)

Description: dried peas are one of the pulses group, and are available whole or as split (half) peas which may be green or yellow.

Properties: an excellent source of starch, vegetable protein, fibre, vitamins (especially B group) and minerals (including iron, magnesium, phosphorus, potassium and manganese). They are extremely low in fat.

Health benefits: supply starch which provides slow-release energy, avoiding peaks of blood glucose, and hence are helpful in prevention and control of diabetes. They provide valuable protein (which is especially useful if eaten with other vegetable proteins) for tissue growth and repair. The peas contain insoluble fibre, which promotes healthy, regular bowel function and may lower the risk of development of diseases of the digestive tract, including cancer. They provide soluble fibre which helps to lower blood cholesterol levels and may protect against heart and circulatory disease. They also supply vitamins and minerals involved in essential metabolic functions, the promotion of good heath and disease prevention.

Cooking/serving methods: best rinsed and soaked in cold water for several hours before boiling in fresh water. The peas become 'mushy' when cooked. They are usually added to soups or vegetarian dishes such as pease pudding.

Disadvantages: may cause wind.

Pecan nuts

Description: oval, crinkly, sweet-tasting nuts of the pecan tree, imported from the southern USA.

Properties: a useful source of vegetable protein and an excellent source of vitamins (including B group and E) and minerals (especially iron, potassium, phosphorus, copper and selenium). They also contain essential fatty acids.

Health benefits: provide protein (especially useful when combined with other vegetable proteins) for tissue growth and repair. The nuts contain vitamins and minerals that are essential for metabolic processes, maintenance of health and prevention of disease. Vitamin E and selenium are especially important due to their antioxidant activity. Pecan nuts provide fatty acids that are necessary for good health.

Cooking/serving methods: may be eaten as whole nuts

or incorporated into sweet or savoury dishes.
Disadvantages: high fat content. Pecan nuts may provoke allergy and can be a choking hazard.

Pepper (black and white)
Description: powder composed of the ground, dried fruits (peppercorns) of a plant native to south Asia, but which is extensively cultivated. Pepper is widely used as a pungent, 'hot' spice in cookery and also for healing in herbal medicine. White pepper comes from the same plant, but the pericarp of the fruit is removed before drying and grinding, whereas with black pepper, the whole fruit is used.
Properties: the active chemicals in black and white pepper are a substance called piperine, a resin known as chavicin, volatile oil, starch and cellulose.
Health benefits: in herbal medicine, pepper is considered to have stimulant, cooling and anti-flatulence activity. It is used to treat digestive problems such as wind and constipation, and also to stimulate a sluggish digestion or to relieve nausea and diarrhoea. It is considered useful in cooling feverish conditions and has also been tried in the treatment of arthritic and paralytic disorders.
Cooking/serving methods: used worldwide to flavour savoury dishes.
Disadvantages: usually none reported.

Peppermint
Description: a herb which grows in damp, marshy conditions and on waste ground in Britain and throughout Europe, the leaves of which are used for healing in herbal medicine. Oil of peppermint is widely used commercially, both in the food industry (e.g. in sweets) and in domestic products such as toothpaste.

Peppers

Properties: contains a volatile oil consisting of several active compounds, including menthol.

Health benefits: in herbal medicine, oil of peppermint is considered to have stimulant, antispasmodic and anti-flatulence properties and is an excellent remedy for digestive and stomach complaints. It is used to treat wind, nausea, indigestion and diarrhoea. Peppermint water is commonly used to raise body temperature and induce perspiration. Peppermint 'tea' can help relieve the symptoms of colds and flu, may calm heart palpitations and is sometimes used to reduce appetite. Since the flavour of peppermint is very strong, it is often administered in combination with other herbs such as elderflower.

Cooking/serving methods: available as a herbal 'tea' from health food shops. Peppermint oil, and preparations and tablets made from it are also in common use.

Disadvantages: some people find the taste of peppermint unpleasant or may have an aversion to the oil.

Peppers (pimientos, sweet, red, green and yellow)

Description: also known as pimientos, these tropical fruits may be green, red or yellow. They are used as vegetables in savoury dishes and salads. They have succulent flesh, and the red and yellow varieties taste sweet.

Properties: contain fibre and carbohydrate and are a rich source of vitamin C, beta carotene (red and yellow varieties are especially good) and plant chemicals such as flavonoids. Peppers are low in calories.

Health benefits: vitamin C is essential for the health of tissues, such as blood vessels, and has anti-infective properties that may boost the immune system and protect against viral infections like the common cold. Beta carotene and flavonoids have powerful antioxidant activity and are believed to help protect against certain diseases, including some forms of cancer.

Cooking/serving methods: stalk ends are removed along with the white ribs and seeds inside the pepper. Peppers may be eaten raw in salads, chopped and incorporated into savoury dishes such as stews and casseroles, or stuffed and baked or grilled.

Disadvantages: usually none reported.

Persimmon (Sharon fruit)

Description: round, bright orange tropical fruits grown in Japan and other hot climates. They slightly resemble large tomatoes but are orange rather than red and usually come with stalk end and brown papery leaves still attached. The skins are leathery and the orange-yellow flesh is sweet and juicy.

Properties: contain fruit sugar, soluble fibre, vitamins (especially C) and minerals (particularly potassium). Excellent source of beta carotene (carotenes).

Health benefits: it provides readily available energy. Soluble fibre helps to lower blood cholesterol levels and may protect the heart and circulation against disease. Insoluble fibre promotes healthy bowel function and may protect against digestive tract disorders, including cancer. Vitamin C and potassium are vitally involved in metabolic activity and in ensuring the health of tissues and organs. Vitamin C is believed to help ward off viral infections such as the common cold. Beta carotene has powerful antioxidant activity and is believed to protect against certain diseases, including some cancers.

Cooking/serving methods: usually eaten as fresh fruit or as part of fruit salad.

Disadvantages: usually none reported.

Pheasant

Pheasant see **Game**

Pigeon see **Game**

Pimientos see **Peppers**

Pineapples

Description: familiar, large, tropical fruits with thick, orange, scaly, segmented skins crowned by a cluster of stiff green leaves. The flesh is bright yellow, sweet, juicy and succulent when ripe. They are eaten and used for healing in traditional medicine.

Properties: contain fruit sugar, fibre and a good source of vitamin C but low in other vitamins and minerals. They contain a powerful natural enzyme, bromelin, which breaks down proteins and has medicinal uses that are continuing to be investigated.

Health benefits: provide readily available energy and fluid. Soluble fibre helps to lower blood cholesterol levels and may protect against heart and circulatory disease. Insoluble fibre promotes healthy bowel function and may help to protect against digestive tract diseases, including cancer. Vitamin C is essential for the health of tissues such as blood vessels, has anti-infective properties and may help to protect against viral infections such as the common cold. Bromelin has been used medicinally to treat arthritis and tissue injuries. It is believed that it may have applications in the treatment of heart and circulatory disease, blocked sinuses and infections of the urinary tract. In traditional medicine, pineapple juice is used as a gargle for sore throats and eating the fruit is held to be beneficial for the relief of arthritis, respiratory tract infections and indigestion.

Cooking/serving methods: fresh pineapple is usually eaten alone or as part of fruit salad. or the fruit may be incorporated into desserts. Commercially produced canned pineapple either in natural juice or syrup, is popular and widely used in similar ways. Canning removes the bromelin but only slightly lowers the vitamin C content.

Disadvantages: rarely, may provoke an allergic reaction which can be severe.

Pine nuts (pine kernels)

Description: creamy white seeds of a tree grown in China and south Asia.

Properties: an excellent source of protein and a good provider of fibre, vitamins (especially B group and E). Pine nuts are high in fat but most of this is in a useful, unsaturated form.

Health benefits: supply valuable protein (especially useful when combined with other vegetable proteins) for tissue growth and repair. They provide fibre which promotes healthy bowel function and may help to prevent diseases of the digestive system, including cancer. Pine nuts are a source of vitamins involved in metabolic functions, health of tissues and organs and disease prevention. They also provide fatty acids that are essential for health.

Cooking/serving methods: can be added to savoury or sweet dishes, bread, cakes, etc.

Disadvantages: high in calories so may need to be used sparingly.

Pinto beans

Description: elongated, creamy-coloured dried beans speckled with reddish spots. They are one of the most popular of the pulses in the USA (where the beans are cultivated) and Latin America. They are pink in colour with an earthy flavour when cooked.

Properties: high in fibre. They are also a good source of

vegetable protein, starch, vitamins (especially B group and E) and minerals (including iron, manganese, phosphorus, magnesium and potassium).

Health benefits: provide soluble fibre which helps to lower blood cholesterol level and they may protect the heart and circulation. They also provide insoluble fibre which promotes healthy bowel function and may help to protect the digestive system against diseases, including cancer. The beans are a useful source of protein (especially when combined with other vegetable proteins) for tissue growth and repair. They supply starch for slow-release energy, which avoids peaks of blood glucose, and hence are helpful in the control and prevention of diabetes. They provide vitamins and minerals that are involved in metabolic functions, maintenance of health and prevention of disease.

Cooking/serving methods: pinto beans should be rinsed and soaked in cold water for several hours or overnight, before being cooked by boiling in fresh water for about one hour. They may be used in a variety of savoury dishes such as casseroles, soups and stews.

Disadvantages: may cause wind.

Pistachio nuts

Description: fruits of a tree native to the Mediterranean region. They have hard, brown shells which enclose olive green-coloured kernels.

Properties: a useful source of protein, vitamins (excellent for E and good for B group) and minerals (especially potassium, iron, phosphorus, copper and selenium). They also contain essential fatty acids.

Health benefits: provide protein (especially useful when combined with other vegetable proteins) for tissue growth and repair. The nuts supply vitamins and minerals that are involved in essential metabolic functions, maintenance of health of tissues and organs, and prevention of disease. Vitamin E and selenium have natural antioxidant properties and may help to prevent diseases, including cancer. Essential fatty acids are necessary for good health, e.g. for cell membranes and nerves.

Cooking/serving methods: eaten on their own or incorporated into savoury and sweet dishes or used as a garnish. They are also available as salted nuts.

Disadvantages: high in fat and calories. They may provoke allergy and can be a choking hazard.

Plantain (common, broad-leaved plantain)

Description: common, wayside weed in Britain and Europe, which has a rosette of broad, stripy leaves and brown flowers borne on an upright stalk. It is used for healing in herbal medicine.

Properties: contains various active substances.

Health benefits: in herbal medicine, plantain is believed to have cooling, astringent and diuretic properties. It is administered as expressed juice, a poultice of leaves or as an ointment or infusion. It may be used to relieve skin inflammation, bites and stings, minor wounds (to promote healing), burns and scalds. Plantain may also be used to relieve fever.

Cooking/serving methods: not applicable.

Disadvantages: usually none reported.

Plums (see also **Prunes**)

Description: familiar, soft, round or oval fruits with central stone, varying in colour from purple to red, yellow or green (greengages). There are many different varieties grown in Britain and many other countries. A popular home-grown variety is the Victoria plum.

Pomegranates

Properties: a good source of fruit sugar, fibre, vitamins (especially C and E), minerals (particularly potassium) and flavonoids.

Health benefits: supply readily available energy and soluble fibre which helps to lower blood cholesterol levels and may protect the heart and circulation. Insoluble fibre promotes healthy bowel function and may help to protect against diseases of the digestive system, including cancer. Plums provide vitamins and minerals that are involved in essential metabolic processes and in the maintenance of health. Vitamins C, E and flavonoids have natural antioxidant activity and are believed to help to protect against disease, including some cancers.

Cooking/serving methods: may be eaten as fresh fruits but are often gently boiled (stewed) and used in desserts. They are also used to make jam, and are available commercially as canned fruit.

Disadvantages: usually none reported.

Pomegranates

Description: exotic fruits of a tree native to Asia but which is widely cultivated. The fruits are pinkish red, about the size of an apple, and have a hard rind. The flesh is bright red, sweet and succulent, and packed around numerous seeds.

Properties: an excellent source of fruit sugar, fibre (from the seeds), vitamins (especially C), minerals (especially potassium) and flavonoids.

Health benefits: provide readily available energy. Soluble fibre helps to lower blood cholesterol levels and may protect the heart and circulation. Insoluble fibre promotes healthy bowel function and may help to prevent diseases of the digestive system, including cancer. Vitamin C has anti-infective and antioxidant properties and is believed to boost the immune system and possibly protect against viral infections such as the common cold. Flavonoids are natural antioxidants which may help to prevent diseases, including some cancers.

Cooking/serving methods: usually eaten as fresh fruits. Pomegranates are processed commercially as an ingredient of fruit juices.

Disadvantages: usually none reported.

Pomelos (pummelos)

Description: unusual, large, exotic, yellow citrus fruit from south-east Asia. They are oval in shape and have yellow, tangy flesh. Grapefruits are derived from them.

Properties: a good source of fibre, vitamins (excellent for C) and minerals (including potassium).

Health benefits: soluble fibre helps to lower blood cholesterol levels and may protect the heart and circulation. Insoluble fibre promotes healthy bowel function and may help to protect against diseases of the digestive system, including cancer. Vitamin C has anti-infective and antioxidant properties and is believed to boost the immune system and possibly protect against viral infections such as the common cold.

Cooking/serving methods: usually eaten as fresh fruit.

Disadvantages: none usually reported.

Porridge see **Oats**

Poultry

Description: meat from domestic fowls – mainly chickens, turkeys, ducks and geese. All poultry are excellent sources of protein, vitamins (especially B group) and minerals (including iron, potassium, phosphorus and zinc). See individual entries.

Potatoes

Description: staple part of the British diet with many different varieties of potato being grown, both commercially and in the garden. Contrary to popular belief, they are not fattening unless cooked in a way that adds fat, such as frying or roasting.

Properties: an excellent source of starch, fibre (especially if skins are eaten), vitamins (especially C) and minerals (particularly potassium).

Health benefits: provide slow-release energy, which avoids peaks of blood sugar levels, and are therefore valuable in the prevention and control of diabetes. Fibre promotes healthy bowel function and may hep to prevent diseases of the digestive system, including cancer. Vitamin C is involved in maintenance of the health of tissues such as blood vessels and has antioxidant and anti-infective activity. It may boost the immune system and possibly helps to protect against viral infections such as the common cold. Potassium is involved in the metabolic regulation of the balance of electrolytes (salts) and water in tissue fluids, and in the correct function of the nervous system.

Cooking/serving methods: may be boiled, baked, roasted or fried. The healthiest way to eat potatoes is boiled or baked with the skins on if grown organically.

Disadvantages: green patches indicate the presence of chemical alkaloids which are poisonous. Potatoes with green patches should not be eaten.

Prawns

Description: popular, small shellfish harvested in British waters and elsewhere. Prawns are one of the types of shellfish most frequently eaten in Britain.

Properties: an excellent source of protein, vitamins (especially B_{12}, also B_1, B_2 and B_3) and minerals (particularly selenium, iodine, calcium and magnesium). They also contain essential fatty acids.

Health benefits: supply first-class protein for tissue growth and repair, and vitamins and minerals that are involved in many metabolic processes, and the maintenance of health and prevention of disease. Selenium has vital antioxidant activity and may help to prevent diseases, including some cancers.

Cooking/serving methods: usually sold as cooked, shelled prawns. May be eaten cold in salads or added to rice dishes, stir fries, etc.

Disadvantages: may provoke allergy. They are a potential cause of food poisoning so should always be refrigerated and eaten fresh.

Prunes

Description: familiar black, wrinkled fruits, which are actually dried plums. They are renowned for their laxative effects. Prunes are available in bags as dried fruit and also canned in juice or syrup.

Properties: rich in fruit sugar, fibre, minerals (especially iron and potassium) and some vitamins (including B_6). They contain natural chemical substances which stimulate activity of the large bowel.

Health benefits: supply readily available energy. They also provide minerals and vitamins that are involved in essential metabolic functions, including maintenance of the health of blood vessels and nerves. Their fibre content and the presence of certain natural chemicals give prunes gentle but effective laxative effect. Eating prunes regularly can relieve constipation and help to restore a natural, regular bowel function. Prune juice is also effective in this way.

Cooking/serving methods: may be eaten dried or soaked, added to fruit salads or cereals or rice pudding.

Pulses

Disadvantages: may cause wind. They are high in calories.

Pulses
Description: a wide variety of dried peas and beans. They are a particularly useful food for vegetarians. All are a good source of vegetable protein, soluble and insoluble fibre, starch, vitamins (especially B group) and minerals (particularly iron, magnesium, manganese, phosphorus and potassium). Pulses include chick peas, haricot beans, kidney beans, lentils and dried peas. See individual entries.

Pumpkins
Description: large, round, orange-yellow-coloured vegetables which are highly popular in the USA and many other countries but eaten less frequently in Britain. Pumpkins have bright orange flesh and are one of the squash family of vegetables. They are also used in herbal medicine.
Properties: contain some carbohydrate and fibre. Pumpkins are an excellent source of vitamins (especially A and E) and minerals (particularly the seeds, which contain iron, potassium, zinc, phosphorus and magnesium). They are also a rich source of beta carotene (carotenes).
Health benefits: provide readily accessible energy. Soluble fibre helps to lower blood cholesterol levels and may protect the heart and circulation. Insoluble fibre promotes healthy bowel function and may protect against diseases of the digestive system, including cancer. Pumpkins supply valuable vitamins and minerals that are involved in metabolic processes, and maintenance of health and prevention of disease. Beta carotene is a precursor of vitamin A and has vital antioxidant activity, combating free radical

damage and possibly protecting against disease, including some cancers. In herbal medicine, pumpkin seeds were used in combination with a purgative to expel parasitic tapeworms. An infusion may also be used to treat urinary disorders and problems relating to an enlarged prostate gland.

Cooking/serving methods: boiled or baked, eaten with other vegetables or made into pies. Pumpkins are readily digestible and may be given as weaning food to babies.

Disadvantages: usually none reported.

Quail see Game

Quince

Description: fruit of a tree native to Persia but cultivated elsewhere. The fruits have tough golden skins and sharp, acidic flesh, and are used for jam making and for healing in herbal medicine. Not commonly available.

Properties: in herbal medicine, quince fruits are used for their astringent and mucilaginous, protective properties.

Health benefits: the fruit is used to prepare a syrup, which protects the digestive system and helps to relieve diarrhoea. A decoction prepared from the seeds may also be used to treat thrush, and inflamed and irritated mucous membranes. Liquid from the fruit may be used to soothe inflamed eyes or skin.

Cooking/serving methods: used to make jams and jellies.

Disadvantages: usually none reported.

Rabbit

Description: skinned, prepared rabbits, which are available in some supermarkets, are usually 'farmed' animals that have been imported. Wild rabbit, sometimes available from rural butchers' shops, is sold as GAME but is less popular than formerly, partly due to the presence of the endemic disease, myxomatosis.

Radishes

Description: although there are several different varieties of radish, the most popular ones are small, spherical and red-skinned with white flesh. Radishes are grown commercially and in home gardens throughout Britain as salad vegetables which have a slightly 'hot' flavour. They are also used for healing in herbal medicine.

Properties: a good source of fibre, vitamins (especially C) and minerals. They contain a volatile oil and several active chemicals, which are useful in herbal medicine.

Health benefits: provide vitamin C, which is essential for the health of various tissues such as blood vessels and for wound healing, and has anti-infective activity, possibly helping to protect against common viral infections such as colds. In herbal medicine, radishes were used to treat and prevent scurvy. They have diuretic properties and are used to treat kidney and urinary complaints, and to prevent the formation of gallstones.

Cooking/serving methods: eaten raw after washing and trimming, or chopped and added to salads.

Disadvantages: usually none reported.

Raisins

Description: several varieties of grape, which are dried, either in the sun or artificially, to produce raisins. These are mainly used in home and commercial baking and confectionery.

Properties: high in sugar and calories; an excellent source of minerals (potassium and iron) and fibre. They are low in fat.

Health benefits: provide readily accessible energy, and minerals that are essential for the maintenance of the health of tissues, including blood cells and the nervous system. Raisins supply fibre which promotes healthy bowel function and may help to protect against diseases of the digestive system, including cancer.

Cooking/serving methods: may be eaten as snacks but are usually used in the baking of cakes, biscuits and puddings.

Disadvantages: high sugar content can contribute to tooth decay and weight gain, if eaten to excess. But raisins are generally regarded as a good provider of energy, minerals and fibre, if eaten in moderation.

Raspberries

Description: popular, bright pink, soft fruits. They grow wild in Scotland but many varieties are cultivated throughout Britain, both commercially and in home gardens. Home-grown raspberries are only available in the summer months but imported fruit may be in supermarkets throughout the year. They are used for healing in natural medicine.

Properties: an excellent source of natural fruit sugar, vitamins (especially C, B$_9$ and E), minerals (rich in potassium) and natural flavonoids called anthocyanidins. They also contain some fibre.

Health benefits: supply readily available energy. They provide vitamins and minerals which are involved in metabolic functions, maintenance of health of tissues such as blood vessels and operation of the nervous system. Vitamin C has natural antioxidant and anti-infective activity and may help to prevent common viral infections such as colds. Anthocyanidins and vitamin E are powerful antioxidants and are believed to help protect against a range of diseases, possibly including some forms of cancer. For maximum health benefits, raspberries are best eaten fresh.

In herbal medicine, raspberry juice (or raspberry juice vinegar) is used to treat digestive complaints and to 'cleanse' the digestive system, to soothe sore throats and feverish illnesses and to treat urinary tract infections such as cystitis. The leaves may be used as a poultice for minor wounds.

Cooking/serving methods: often eaten as fresh fruit or used as a topping for desserts. Raspberries may be added to fruit salad or stewed gently, and are used in home and commercial jam making. They are also available as canned fruit (in which vitamin C level is reduced) and frozen in boxes. Raspberries freeze well (although they become soft when defrosted) and do not lose their vitamin content.

Disadvantages: usually none reported.

Raspberry leaf 'tea'

Description: a herbal 'tea' made from dried, raspberry leaves which has long been used for healing in herbal medicine. Some modern varieties are flavoured with raspberry extract so that they taste of the fruit.

Properties: has mildly astringent and tonic activity due to the presence of certain plant chemicals.

Health benefits: in herbal medicine, the 'tea' is used to treat female reproductive complaints such as period pains. Taken in late pregnancy, it is believed to ease labour and reduce the risk of excessive blood loss after childbirth. It is also used to ease mild digestive upset, diarrhoea and constipation and to relieve similar colicky complaints in babies and young children. Its mild, astringent properties make it suitable for use as a gargle for sore throats, mouth ulcers or as a general mouthwash.

Cooking/serving methods: used as a herbal 'tea'.

Disadvantages: in view of its possible effects on the female reproductive organs, it should be avoided during early pregnancy due to a slight risk of miscarriage.

Red cabbage

Description: a variety of cabbage with purple-red leaves, most frequently used pickled. See CABBAGE.

Redcurrants

Description: small, bright, pinky-red berries borne in clusters on fruit bushes and related to blackcurrants. They are grown less frequently than blackcurrants and not so readily available, although they may be cultivated in gardens. They are grown commercially and used to make redcurrant jelly – a traditional accompaniment for meat.

Properties: a good source of natural fruit sugar, fibre, vitamins (rich in C) and minerals (excellent for potassium and contain iron). Redcurrants also contain flavonoids (anthocyanidins).

Health benefits: supply readily available energy and vitamins and minerals that are involved in vital metabolic activities and maintenance of the health of tissues and organs, including blood vessels and the nervous system. Vitamin C has antioxidant and anti-infective activity, boosts wound healing and may help to protect against common viral infections such as colds. Natural flavonoids in redcurrants also have antioxidant activity and may protect against a range of diseases, including some cancers. Soluble fibre helps to lower blood cholesterol levels and may protect the heart and circulation. Insoluble fibre

Red wine

promotes healthy bowel function and may help to
protect the digestive system against diseases, including
cancer.

Cooking/serving methods: may be eaten raw but their
sharp taste means they are often gently stewed with
sugar. They are mainly used to make jams and jellies.

Disadvantages: usually none reported.

Red wine

Description: red wines are made from a large number
of different varieties of grape and from many
countries of the world. They are widely available in
Britain, offering a wide choice of flavours to suit
almost every taste. There is growing evidence that a
modest consumption of red wine each day is
beneficial for health. Modest consumption means
one to two small glasses each day for women and
two to three for men.

Properties: one bottle of red wine contains 8–14 per
cent alcohol (6 to 10 1/2 units) or 1 to 3 units per
glass. Natural chemicals (polyphenols and other
substances) and small amounts of vitamins and
minerals are also present.

Health benefits: chemicals in red wine are natural
antioxidants which may help to protect against
disease, if taken in moderation. At this level, there
is evidence that there may be protection against
heart and circulatory disease in middle and older
age, reducing the risk of heart attack and
atherosclerosis. Red wine has been shown to slightly
'thin' the blood, reducing the tendency for clots to
form. If drunk with a meal, red wine may aid
digestion. It can enhance a sense of relaxation and
happiness, if used sensibly.

Cooking/serving methods: red wine may be used in
cooking, particularly as a marinade for meat and game.

Disadvantages: as with all alcoholic drinks, there is a risk of abuse. The benefits of red wine disappear if it is consumed at a higher level than that outlined above when it can, over time, cause damage, particularly to the heart and liver. Guidelines issued by the Department of Health advise that a safe upper limit for weekly alcohol consumption is 14 units for women and 21 units for men. A small glass of red wine is equivalent to one unit. It is further advised that 'binge' drinking of the whole weekly 'allowance' during a weekend is damaging to health. Pregnant women are advised not to drink alcohol at all, especially during the first three months of pregnancy, due to the risk of damage to their developing baby.

Rhubarb

Description: familiar 'fruit' with long, pink-green stems and a sharp flavour. Rhubarb is, in fact, a vegetable. It was introduced into Britain in the 18th century and grows readily in gardens and also 'wild' on marginal land. It is available commercially as canned fruit.

Properties: used for healing in herbal medicine. Rhubarb contains oxalic acid, a good source of vitamin C, potassium, manganese and fibre. In large quantities, it has a gentle laxative effect and can stimulate digestion.

Health benefits: provides vitamins and minerals that are involved in metabolic processes and essential for the health of tissues and organs. Soluble fibre helps to lower blood cholesterol levels and may protect the heart and circulation. Insoluble fibre stimulates regular bowel function and may help to protect against diseases of the digestive system including cancer. In herbal medicine, rhubarb is used to relieve digestive complaints, including diarrhoea.

Rice

Cooking/serving methods: needs to be oven-cooked or stewed with sugar as it is naturally sour. Rhubarb may be eaten on its own or with other cooked fruit as a dessert.

Disadvantages: contains oxalic acid and should be avoided by people suffering from gout, arthritis or kidney stones as may exacerbate these conditions. Rhubarb should not be cooked in aluminium saucepans as the acid may leach the mineral from the pan into the fruit and this may be harmful. Rhubarb leaves are poisonous.

Rice

Description: one of the major cereal crops. Rice is the staple food of more than half the world's people. There are many different varieties but all rice is more nutritious if the bran and germ of the grain is retained. However, some types of highly refined, white rice have vitamins and minerals added to them. Rice is also used for healing in traditional medicine.

Properties: all types of rice offer an excellent source of starch and contain protein. Brown rice is a good source of fibre, vitamins (including B group) and minerals (iron, calcium and phosphorus). Parboiled white rice (partly boiled before milling) retains most vitamins, including B_1, which is lost through refining. Rice does not contain gluten.

Health benefits: provides slow-release energy, avoiding peaks of blood glucose, and is therefore useful in the control and prevention of diabetes. It supplies vitamins and minerals (depending upon type) involved in metabolic functions, maintenance of the health of tissues and organs, and disease prevention. Fibre in brown rice promotes healthy bowel function and may help to prevent diseases of the digestive system, including cancer (see also disadvantages).

Rice supplies some protein (the amount depends upon the type of rice), which is especially beneficial when combined with other vegetable proteins, for tissue growth and repair. It is a valuable cereal for those who cannot tolerate gluten, such as people with coeliac disease.

In traditional, herbal medicine, rice is used to settle digestive problems, sickness and diarrhoea. It is an ideal food for anyone recovering from a bout of sickness as it is soothing and non-irritant. Rice water is used to treat feverish and inflammatory conditions such as digestive complaints, cystitis and urinary tract problems. Powdered rice flour or rice starch may be applied as a poultice to wounds, burns and irritated skin.

Cooking/serving methods: usually boiled or part-boiled and fried. Rice is incorporated into or used as a base for a wide variety of savoury (and some sweet) dishes, especially in Eastern and Asian cuisine. Pudding rice is baked with milk to make a dessert.

Disadvantages: rice bran, contained in brown rice, incorporates phytic acid and other anti-nutritional factors which hinder the absorption of calcium and iron from the gut. Hence excessive intake of brown rice may not be helpful. Polished white rice is low in vitamins and people who subsist mainly on this are often deficient in B_1.

Roe (fish roe)

Description: reproductive organs of certain species of fish, usually of cod. 'Hard roe' containing eggs is from the female fish and soft roe (milt), is from the male.

Properties: a good source of protein, vitamins (including B_{12}), minerals (including iron) and omega-3 fatty acids. Roe is also high in cholesterol.

Root vegetables

Health benefits: supplies protein for tissue growth and repair. Vitamins and minerals found in roe are involved in vital metabolic functions and are essential for good health. Omega-3 fatty acids of the type found in roe protect the heart and circulation and reduce the risk of serious diseases such as atherosclerosis, heart attack and stroke.

Cooking/serving methods: 'hard roe' may be sold ready boiled or smoked. Roe is cooked by boiling and may then be cut into slices and fried.

Disadvantages: high in cholesterol and hence may not be suitable for those with high blood cholesterol levels.

Root vegetables

Description: comprise some of the most popular and familiar varieties eaten in Britain such as carrots, potatoes, turnips, swedes, parsnips and beetroot. All are highly nutritious since they are good sources of carbohydrate (starch), vitamins, minerals and fibre. See individual entries.

Rosehips (syrup and 'tea')

Description: bright orange-red fruits of the dog rose – a wild rose with pinky white blooms, which grows in hedgerows throughout the British Isles. The rosehips are used to make a syrup and also crushed and dried to make a herbal 'tea'.

Properties: rich in vitamin C Rosehip syrup was used as a source of this vitamin for British children during the Second World War.

Health benefits: vitamin C is involved in maintaining the health of connective tissue, cartilage, blood vessels, etc. It has antioxidant and anti-infective activity and is believed to boost the immune system, promote healing of wounds and possibly help to prevent common viral infections such as colds.

Cooking/serving methods: to make syrup, the hips are boiled, crushed and sieved to remove the numerous seeds. The liquid is strained and boiled with sugar to make a concentrated syrup, which can then be diluted as a drink. For herbal 'tea', the hips are dried and finely ground.

Disadvantages: rosehip syrup has a high sugar content, which can contribute to tooth decay.

Rosemary

Description: a herb native to the Mediterranean which has been cultivated in Britain for many centuries. It is used in cookery and also in herbal medicine.

Properties: contains several active compounds, which in herbal medicine are said to have tonic, stimulant and astringent properties.

Health benefits: believed to have a beneficial effect on the digestive and nervous systems and is used to relieve digestive upsets, headaches, neuralgia, nervous complaints and feverish colds. Applied externally to the scalp, oil of rosemary is said to prevent baldness and be an effective treatment for dandruff. It is used to soothe skin, and muscle aches and pains when applied as an oil or liniment.

Cooking/serving methods: the dried or fresh herb is used to flavour savoury dishes, traditionally those containing lamb or chicken.

Disadvantages: none usually reported.

Rowan berries

Description: bright red berries from the Rowan or Mountain Ash tree, which grows in upland regions of Britain. They are usually used to make a tangy jelly to accompany meat dishes but also used for healing in herbal medicine.

Royal jelly

Properties: an excellent source of vitamin C. The berries also contain other active substances said to promote healing.

Health benefits: vitamin C is essential for the health of connective tissue, blood vessels, etc., and is thought to boost the immune system and promote healing of wounds. It has antioxidant and anti-infective properties and may help to prevent common viral infections such as colds. In herbal medicine, the juice may be used as an astringent gargle for sore throats and tonsillitis. An infusion of the fruit may be given as a treatment for haemorrhoids. In the 19th century, the berries were given as a country remedy against scurvy.

Cooking/serving methods: used to make a jelly for meat dishes and also for wine and other alcoholic drinks.

Disadvantages: usually none reported.

Royal jelly

Description: a creamy substance, produced by worker bees from their salivary glands and fed exclusively to the few larvae destined to become queen bees. These bees grow to twice the size of ordinary worker honey bees and may live for as long as six years, in comparison to the six-week lifespan of the workers. For these reasons, royal jelly has been hailed as a 'miracle' substance that can heal and help a range of human ailments. There is, however no scientific basis for these claims. Royal jelly is available as a 'health food' supplement, as a yellowish liquid or in capsules, and also as an ingredient of skin products.

Properties: contains vitamins (B group, C), minerals (potassium, sodium and iron) and essential amino acids and fatty acids, all in minute amounts.

Health benefits: in alternative medicine, royal jelly may be used to treat a range of ailments, including lack of energy, myalgic encephalomyelitis (ME), arthritis, skin complaints, failure to thrive in infants, athersoclerosis (hardening of the arteries), anaemia, high blood pressure and depression. Many people claim to feel better and to notice improvements after taking the substance, although there is, as yet, no scientific evidence to support these claims.

Cooking/serving methods: not applicable.

Disadvantages: usually none reported but the cost of royal jelly is high.

Runner beans

Description: popular, garden vegetables with long, fairly coarse, green pods enclosing small, pink, kidney-shaped beans. They are grown throughout the British Isles and are available in summer and early autumn.

Properties: a good source of fibre, vitamins (B9 and C), minerals (including iron) and phytochemicals.

Health benefits: soluble fibre helps to lower blood cholesterol levels and may protect the heart and circulation. Insoluble fibre promotes regular bowel function and may help to prevent diseases of the digestive system, including cancer. Vitamins and minerals are involved in essential metabolic functions, ensuring the health of tissues and organs, and possibly helping to prevent disease. Natural plant chemicals have antioxidant activity and are believed to have a protective effect.

Cooking/serving methods: the 'string' (fibre) around the long edges of the bean pods is removed and the ends are cut off. The pods are eaten thinly sliced lengthways and lightly boiled. Young pods may also be sliced and added to salads.

Disadvantages: usually none reported.

Rye

Description: a cereal that is widely cultivated in Europe

and North America. The flour is used to make a heavy type of bread, which is more popular in Europe than in Britain and also used in crispbreads. In North America, rye is distilled to make whiskey and the cereal is also used as feed for domestic animals.

Properties: contains fibre, carbohydrate, protein, vitamins (especially B group) and minerals (including iron).

Health benefits: supplies a range of nutrients that are essential for health, including carbohydrate for energy and vitamins and minerals involved in vital metabolic activities and the maintenance of cells, tissues and organs.

Cooking/serving methods: in Britain, usually eaten in manufactured foods such as crispbreads.

Disadvantages: contains gluten so must be avoided by those suffering from coeliac disease or gluten intolerance.

Safflower oil

Description: a vegetable oil obtained from the pressed seeds of a plant native to Asia and widely cultivated. The oil is used for cooking and also in other products such as cosmetics and paints.

Properties: an excellent source of polyunsaturated fats, including essential fatty acids and vitamin E.

Health benefits: supplies essential fatty acids necessary for good health, which are involved in vital metabolic processes and form components of cells and natural chemicals. Vitamin E has antioxidant activity and may help to protect against disease. Safflower oil may protect the heart and circulation, and possibly be beneficial in the treatment of inflammatory conditions such as arthritis, eczema and psoriasis.

Cooking/serving methods: may be used for stir fries, etc. or in salad dressing.

Disadvantages: high in calories It should be eaten sparingly as part of a low-fat diet.

Saffron
Description: originally an exotic spice from Persia (now Iran) and the East, which is also widely cultivated throughout Europe. Parts of the dried flowers (stigmas) are used as a spice to colour foods yellow and to give a delicate flavour. It is also used for healing in herbal medicine. It was traditionally believed to be an aphrodisiac.
Properties: contains a volatile oil and several active chemicals said to have healing properties.
Health benefits: in herbal medicine, saffron is administered as a tincture (a medicine) or powder to relieve menstrual and menopausal problems. It is also used to treat neuralgia, feverishness in children, diarrhoea and depression.
Cooking/serving methods: used as a spice, e.g. in rice dishes.
Disadvantages: usually none reported but saffron is a very costly spice.

Sage (common sage)
Description: a herb that is native to the northern Mediterranean but which is extensively cultivated throughout Europe and in the British Isles. It is used as a herb to flavour food and for healing in herbal medicine.
Properties: contains a volatile oil and several compounds said to have stimulant, astringent and tonic properties, and the ability to calm a disordered digestion.
Health benefits: in herbal medicine, sage may be administered as a herbal 'tea', infusion, essential oil or poultice. It is used as a gargle for sore throats and tonsillitis. Sage 'tea' may relieve nervous complaints,

hysteria and feverish excitement. It is valued as a tonic for nervous system and stomach complaints and to relieve wind and indigestion. An infusion may relieve the symptoms of colds, measles, headaches and tiredness. Fresh leaves rubbed on to the teeth and gums can cleanse and soothe them. Oil of sage may help to ease rheumatism and aches and pains, and the leaves may be applied as a poultice.

Cooking/serving methods: the fresh or dried herb is used to flavour food, especially meat dishes such as pork.

Disadvantages: usually none reported.

Salmon

Description: prized for many years in Britain as the 'king of fish', numbers of wild, Atlantic salmon have slumped alarmingly in recent years and stringent conservation strategies are now in place. Paradoxically, the farming of salmon has made the fish more widely available (and affordable) although the practice has raised considerable concern among environmental and conservation organisations. Almost all of the salmon available in Britain is farmed fish but wild Pacific salmon are imported frozen since their numbers have remained high They can be obtained from some supermarkets. All salmon are oily fish with succulent, pink, 'meaty' flesh. Commercially produced smoked and canned salmon is also available.

Properties: an excellent source of protein, vitamins (especially B_{12}, A and D) minerals (including iodine) and omega-3 fatty acids.

Health benefits: supply first-class protein for tissue growth and repair, and vitamins and minerals involved in vital metabolic activities and maintenance of health. Regular consumption of oily fish, such as salmon, reduces the risk of heart and circulatory disease and may improve symptoms of psoriasis and arthritis in some people. Omega-3 fatty acids are vital for the development of the brain and nervous system of a foetus, and pregnant women are especially advised to include oily fish in their diet. Health experts recommend eating oily fish three times each week in order to protect against cardiovascular disease.

Cooking/serving methods: fresh salmon may be poached, baked or grilled and eaten either hot or cold, or incorporated into savoury dishes. Smoked salmon is ready cooked and usually eaten cold with salad, etc.

Disadvantages: rarely, may provoke allergy.

Sardines

Description: small, silver, oily marine fish, sometimes available fresh but more commonly canned in vegetable oil, brine or tomato sauce.

Properties: an excellent source of protein, vitamins (especially A, B_{12} and D) minerals (particularly iron and zinc) and omega-3 fatty acids.

Health benefits: provide first-class protein for tissue growth and repair, and vitamins and minerals involved in vital metabolic activities and maintenance of health. Regular consumption of oily fish, including sardines, reduces the risk of heart and circulatory disease and may improve symptoms of psoriasis and arthritis in some people. Omega-3 fatty acids are vital for foetal development of the brain and nervous system, and pregnant women are advised to include oily fish in their diet. Health experts recommend that everyone should eat oily fish three times each week in order to protect against cardiovascular disease.

Cooking/serving methods: fresh sardines are often grilled and served on toast. Canned fish are 'ready to eat' and may be served hot or cold or incorporated into savoury dishes.

Satsumas

Disadvantages: rarely, may provoke allergy.

Satsumas
Description: familiar citrus fruit grown in Spain and Morocco, with pale orange, loose skin, sometimes with greenish tinge, that peels easily. The flesh is sweet and succulent. The fruits don't have pips and are therefore popular with children.
Properties: provide fruit sugar and are an excellent source of vitamin C, soluble fibre (pectin) and flavonoids.
Health benefits: supply readily available energy. Vitamin C is necessary for the health of connective tissue, blood vessels, etc., promotes wound healing, and has antioxidant and anti-infective activity. Vitamin C may also help to protect against common viral infections such as colds and may boost the immune system. Soluble fibre (contained in membranes and white, stringy pith) may help to lower blood cholesterol levels and reduce the risk of heart and circulatory disease. Antioxidant flavonoids and vitamin C may help to lessen the risk of other diseases, including some forms of cancer.
Cooking/serving methods: eaten as fresh fruit.
Disadvantages: usually none reported.

Saw palmetto berries
Description: fruit of a bush native to the North Atlantic coast of the USA and southern California. The berries have long been used for healing in traditional medicine and recent medical trials have tended to confirm their therapeutic use on urinary problems caused by an enlarged prostate gland. Scientists have begun to identify the ways in which compounds contained in the berries may work at cellular level. The berries are available as a supplement.
Properties: diuretic, tonic and sedative.

Health benefits: in men suffering from an enlarged prostate gland, saw palmetto extract may stimulate complete emptying of the bladder and reduce the frequency of urination so that the sufferer feels better. Some studies suggest that compounds in the berries act at enzyme level to inhibit the proliferation of prostate gland cells, which leads to enlargement. In herbal medicine, extract of saw palmetto is also used to ease chronic catarrh and respiratory symptoms and to promote tissue building.

Cooking/serving methods: not applicable.

Disadvantages: at high daily doses, saw palmetto berries may cause slight stomach upset but these symptoms are rare.

Scallops

Description: shellfish with large, whitish brown deeply ribbed, fluted shells. The flesh is firm and white with orange-pink 'coral'. Scallops are harvested in British waters. They are usually sold open and ready-cleaned or may be cooked.

Properties: an excellent source of protein, vitamins (especially B_{12} and B_3), minerals (particularly selenium, potassium and zinc; also iodine, magnesium and calcium). They also contain essential fatty acids.

Health benefits: provide protein for tissue growth and repair, and vitamins and minerals involved in vital metabolic processes and in the maintenance of health. Selenium has powerful antioxidant activity and may help to prevent disease, including some cancers. It is able to bind and remove poisonous heavy metal compounds. Essential fatty acids of the type found in shellfish protect the heart and circulation and may help to prevent disease.

Cooking/serving methods: scallops are usually sold ready

opened and cleaned. They may be lightly boiled,
steamed, baked, grilled or fried and should be eaten
on the day of purchase or when absolutely fresh.

Disadvantages: shellfish are a well-known cause of food
poisoning and must be eaten fresh. Scallops are a
common cause of allergy and should be avoided by
people suffering from gout.

Seaweed

Description: various species of seaweed, such as laver,
which is common around British shores, are both
edible and nutritious. However, it is vital to ensure
that the beach and sea where the seaweed is
collected are free from (sewage) pollution. Seaweed
is also available in tablet form from health stores.

Properties: all seaweeds are an excellent source of
minerals (especially iodine; also sodium iron, calcium
copper, zinc, magnesium and potassium) and contain
some vitamins (B group including B_{12} and vitamin
A). Also contain beta carotene (carotenes).

Health benefits: provides useful minerals and vitamins
that are involved in vital metabolic processes and in
the maintenance of health. Beta carotene has
powerful antioxidant activity and may help to prevent
diseases, including some cancers.

Cooking/serving methods: fresh seaweed should be
thoroughly washed in clean, running fresh water and
may be boiled or steamed as a vegetable. In Ireland
and Wales, laver is made into savoury flat rissoles –
laver cakes – which are coated in oatmeal and fried.
In Chinese and Japanese cookery, dried seaweed is
used extensively in soups and other dishes to flavour
food.

Disadvantages: most seaweed is high in sodium and may
be unsuitable for people suffering from certain
medical conditions. It may be contaminated with

pollutants so should only be gathered from a source known to be clean.

Seeds
Description: a number of different types of seeds, which are commonly used in a variety of ways in cookery. The most popular types include pine kernels, pumpkin, sesame and sunflower seeds (see individual entries). All are good sources of vegetable protein and oils (polyunsaturated fats), vitamins (B group and E), some minerals and fibre.

Semolina see **Wheat**

Sesame seeds
Description: tiny, oil-bearing seeds of a plant native to tropical Asia. They are widely used in food manufacturing, e.g. in breads and biscuits, and in vegetarian and Middle Eastern cuisine. The oil is also extracted commercially and used as a cooking oil. The seeds have nutty flavour.
Properties: an excellent source of protein, fibre, polyunsaturated oils, vitamins (especially E and B group) and minerals (particularly calcium).
Health benefits: provide protein for tissue growth and repair. Fibre promotes regular bowel function and may help to prevent diseases of the digestive system, including some cancers. They also supply polyunsaturated fats that are essential for health and which may help to lower blood cholesterol levels, if eaten in moderation. Sesame seeds provide vitamins and minerals valuable for good health and protection against disease.
Cooking/serving methods: may be eaten plain or roasted, added to vegetarian or other savoury and sweet dishes. They are used to make a Turkish sweetmeat

Shallots

called Halva – a form of honey and seed cake – and the creamy sauce called tahini. The seeds are often used as a coating on bread or are toasted and sprinkled onto cereal.

Disadvantages: high in calories.

Shallots

Description: less common members of the onion family, with small bulbs covered by brown, papery skin. They are popular in French cuisine to flavour sauces, etc. Have a slightly garlic-like flavour. Their properties are the same as those for other members of the onion family.

Shellfish

Description: various species of molluscs and crustaceans that have been a valuable food source of people throughout the world for thousands of years. Popular types in Britain include prawns, shrimps, crabs, lobsters, oysters, whelks, scallops, cockles and mussels. (See individual entries.) All are excellent sources of protein, vitamins (B group and E), minerals (selenium, iodine, zinc, magnesium and calcium) and contain valuable essential fatty acids, like those present in oily fish.

Shrimps

Description: smallest form of shellfish, resembling miniature prawns. Usually sold ready-boiled in their shells when they are pink, and also available canned and potted.

Properties: an excellent source of protein, vitamins (especially B group and E), minerals (particularly selenium, iodine, zinc, magnesium and calcium) and some essential fatty acids.

Health benefits: provide valuable protein for tissue

growth and repair. They also supply a range of valuable vitamins and minerals that are involved in essential metabolic functions and the maintenance of health of tissues and organs. Vitamin E and selenium are powerful antioxidants which may help to prevent certain diseases including some cancers. Eating shrimps may help to lower blood cholesterol levels and the essential fatty acids they contain may help to protect against heart and circulatory disease.

Cooking/serving methods: raw shrimps are grey-brown in colour. They should be rinsed in clear, running cold water and then cooked by boiling in fresh water for about five minutes. When cool, the shells can be gently pulled off. Usually served cold as 'starters' in salads or seafood cocktails or hot in rice dishes, curries, soups, sauces, etc.

Disadvantages: like all shellfish, shrimps may provoke allergy. They are susceptible to bacterial contamination and should be eaten as fresh as possible to avoid the risk of food poisoning. They should only be obtained from a reputable source.

Skate

Description: fairly large, flat fish with brown-grey skin, related to rays. The diamond-shaped 'wings' are sold for food and these have pinkish white flesh and prominent radiating bones.

Properties: an excellent source of protein, vitamins (especially B_{12}) and minerals (including iron). It is low in fat.

Health benefits: provide first-class protein for tissue growth and repair, and vitamins and minerals essential for health.

Cooking/serving methods: poached, baked, grilled or fried and served with vegetables or incorporated into a fish dish.

Sloe berries

Disadvantages: bones may be a choking hazard. Rarely, may provoke allergy.

Sloe berries
Description: small, dusky, blue-purple fruits of the blackthorn tree, which grows wild in various parts of Britain. The bitter fruits containing small stones are used to make a jelly, or added with sugar to gin to make the home-made liquor, sloe gin.
Properties: a good source of vitamins, minerals and flavonoids.
Health benefits: supply vitamins, minerals and natural antioxidants that are essential for the health of tissues and organs, and for prevention of disease.
Cooking/serving methods: may be boiled with sugar and the liquid strained to make a sharp-tasting jelly to accompany meat. Also, whole washed fruit can be added with sugar to gin to make sloe gin.
Disadvantages: usually none reported.

Sole
Description: three species of flatfish – common, lemon and Dover – all with brown to olive-green mottled, slimy skin, and white, delicately flavoured flesh. Usually available as fillets but sometimes as whole fish.
Properties: an excellent source of protein, vitamins (especially B_{12}) and minerals (including iron). It is very low in fat.
Health benefits: provides first-class protein for tissue growth and repair, and vitamins and minerals that are essential for good health and the prevention of disease.
Cooking/serving methods: baked, poached, grilled or fried and served with vegetables or incorporated into fish dishes.

Disadvantages: rarely, may cause allergy.

Soya beans
Description: probably the most well-known and versatile of the pulses, but for the food products made from the beans rather than the beans themselves. Soya beans are widely used in many manufactured foods, from ready-made vegetarian meals to baby milk. The beans are creamy yellow in colour and slightly oily when cooked.

Properties: a good source of high-quality protein containing many necessary amino acids, unlike most pulses. They are also an excellent source of starch, fibre, vitamins (B group – B, B$_6$, B$_9$ and E), minerals (especially potassium, iron, phosphorus, manganese and magnesium) and phytochemicals including plant oestrogens. Soya beans are fairly high in unsaturated fats.

Health benefits: supply protein for tissue growth and repair. Starch provides slow-release energy, avoiding peaks of blood glucose, and hence it is useful for the control and possible prevention of diabetes. Insoluble fibre promotes regular bowel function and may help to protect against diseases of the digestive system, including cancer. Soluble fibre helps to lower blood cholesterol levels and may help to protect against heart and circulatory disease. Soya beans provide essential vitamins and minerals involved in many metabolic functions and the maintenance of the health of tissues and organs. Vitamin E has antioxidant activity and may help to protect against various diseases, including cancer. Phyto-oestrogens in soya beans may help to protect women against breast and other cancers and may help to relieve menopausal symptoms. They also may help to reduce the risk of osteoporosis.

Spinach

Cooking/serving methods: dried beans should be thoroughly rinsed and soaked overnight in cold water before cooking, by boiling for one to two hours. They may be used in a variety of vegetarian and other dishes. Products made from soya beans include flour, milk, oil, soya cheese, bean curd, tofu, soya sauce, vegetarian burgers, sausages, 'mince' and spreads. Soya products can be a valuable resource for infants and others allergic to cows' milk and dairy products.

Disadvantages: a fairly common cause of migraines and allergy. Many manufactured soya foods contain high levels of salt.

Spinach

Description: vegetable with soft green leaves and stalks, which tends to have a soggy texture and strong 'mineral' flavour when cooked. Although the health benefits of spinach have long been recognized, and it is now thought to be one of the vegetables that may prevent cancer, it is not always popular as a food choice. It is used for healing in herbal medicine.

Properties: an excellent source of fibre, vitamins (C, A and B_9), minerals (especially potassium also iron and many others) and carotenes (including beta carotene and carotenoid pigments).

Health benefits: particularly valued for its mineral, carotene and carotenoid content. The minerals in spinach are believed to be beneficial in aiding recovery after illness and in the treatment of anaemia, hypertension (high blood pressure) and constipation. The carotenes and carotenoids in spinach are powerful antioxidants and may protect against various forms of cancer and other diseases, including age-related blindness in the elderly. Folate (B_9) in spinach helps to reduce the risk of neural tube defects (spina bifida) in a developing foetus. In herbal medicine, spinach is used as convalescence food and to treat anaemia and vitamin C deficiency.

Cooking/serving methods: may be washed and eaten raw with other salad greens or lightly steamed or boiled and eaten as a vegetable. Spinach may also be incorporated into many other dishes and used in food manufacturing.

Disadvantages: contains oxalic acid which, if consumed in large quantities, may interfere with absorption of iron and calcium. In susceptible people, oxalic acid may encourage the formation of kidney and bladder stones.

Split peas see **Peas (dried)**

Sprats
Description: small, silver, oily marine fish, usually cooked whole once gutted. They are also available as smoked fish and canned in tomato sauce, oil or brine.

Properties: an excellent source of protein, vitamins (B_{12}, A and D) minerals (potassium, iodine, iron and calcium) and omega-3 fatty acids.

Health benefits: supply first-class protein for tissue growth and repair. Vitamins and minerals in sprats are involved in a wide range of metabolic functions and in the maintenance of health. Omega-3 fatty acids in fish oils may help to improve skin conditions such as psoriasis and help to reduce the risk of heart and circulatory disease.

Cooking/serving methods: usually fried or grilled.

Disadvantages: rarely, may cause allergy.

Spring greens
Description: a variety of cabbage with tender green

Spring onions

leaves containing many health-enhancing nutrients. See CABBAGE.

Spring onions

Description: a form of small, salad onion, the bulb and stalk of which are eaten raw. See ONIONS.

Squashes

Description: varieties of vegetable, which include pumpkins, acorn and butternut squashes, usually with bright orange, slightly sweet-tasting flesh. All are excellent sources of antioxidant beta carotene and other vitamins (A and E) and minerals (potassium, iron, zinc and magnesium). See individual entries.

Star anise (Chinese anise)

Description: a star-shaped, dried fruit used as a spice and for healing in herbal medicine. It has an aromatic, aniseed flavour and is used in Chinese cookery.

Properties: contains an aromatic volatile oil and several active compounds.

Health benefits: in herbal medicine, it is used to relieve wind, colic and griping pains. It may also be used to clear catarrh in chest infections.

Cooking/serving methods: used as a spice in oriental cookery.

Disadvantages: none usually reported.

Star fruit

Description: exotic, green-yellow, tropical fruit with sweet, fragrant succulent flesh. Sometimes available in supermarkets.

Properties: a good source of fruit sugar, fibre, vitamins (especially C) and minerals.

Health benefits: provides readily accessible energy. Soluble fibre helps to lower blood cholesterol levels and may lessen the risk of heart and circulatory disease. Insoluble fibre promotes healthy bowel function and may protect against diseases of the digestive system, including cancer. Vitamin C is vital for the health of connective tissue, blood vessels, etc. and has anti-infective and antioxidant activity, aiding wound-healing and possibly guarding against diseases and infections such as the common cold.

Cooking/serving methods: eaten as fresh fruit and as a garnish for desserts.

Disadvantages: none usually reported.

Steak see **Beef**

Strawberries

Description: popular fruits associated with sunny, summer days. Several varieties of strawberry grow readily throughout most of Britain and they are also imported. They are available canned and are widely used in food manufacturing. Strawberries have long been valued for healing in herbal medicine.

Properties: a source of fruit sugar and excellent for vitamin C. They are low in calories.

Health benefits: vitamin C is essential for the health of connective tissue, blood vessels, ligaments, etc., and it promotes wound healing and is believed to boost the immune system. It has antioxidant activity and may help to protect against various diseases, including some cancers. It may also help to protect against viral infections, including the common cold. In herbal medicine, strawberries were used to treat gout, rheumatic and arthritic complaints and eye inflammation. They were rubbed on teeth to remove discolouration, on the face to relieve sunburn, and were also used to freshen and whiten the skin.

Sultanas

Cooking/serving methods: usually eaten as fresh fruits or used as toppings on deserts. They may also be gently boiled and eaten as stewed fruit.

Disadvantages: a relatively common cause of allergy in the form of hives (an itchy rash). Strawberries contain salicylates and should be avoided by people who cannot take aspirin (which contains the related compound, salicylic acid). The fine seeds on the outside of strawberries may cause irritation in people suffering from colitis and related bowel disorders.

Sultanas

Description: particular varieties of dried grape, usually light brown in colour, and used in home and commercial baking for cakes, biscuits, cereal bars, etc.

Properties: an excellent source of fibre and minerals (especially iron and potassium). They are high in natural sugar.

Health benefits: provide readily accessible energy due to their high sugar content. They supply valuable minerals involved in a variety of essential metabolic functions and maintenance of the health of tissues and organs. Fibre promotes healthy bowel function and may protect against diseases and disorders of the digestive system, including cancer.

Cooking/serving methods: used as an ingredient in cakes, biscuits, cereals, etc. and as a snack food.

Disadvantages: high sugar content may cause tooth decay.

Sunflower seeds and oil

Description: the greyish brown seeds of sunflowers are used in vegetarian cookery and processed commercially for their oil, which is widely used for frying, salad dressings, etc. It is also used to make sunflower margarine.

Properties: an excellent source of protein, fibre, vitamins (B group, but not B$_{12}$, and E) and minerals. High in unsaturated fatty acids, including linoleic acid.

Health benefits: supply protein (complete if eaten with other vegetable proteins), which is used for tissue growth and repair. Fibre encourages healthy bowel function and may help to prevent diseases of the digestive system, including cancer. Vitamins and minerals are involved in a wide range of metabolic functions and in the maintenance of good health. Vitamin E has antioxidant activity and may help to lessen the risk of certain diseases occurring, including some cancers. Fatty acids such as linoleic acid are necessary components of cell membranes and have important roles within the body.

Cooking/serving methods: may be added to breakfast cereals, baked goods and vegetarian dishes. Oil is widely used for stir-frying, etc.

Disadvantages: high in calories.

Swedes

Description: familiar, purple-brown, large, round root vegetables with yellow, slightly sweet flesh when cooked. They are grown throughout Britain for human consumption and for animal food.

Properties: a good source of fibre, vitamin C and phytochemicals (indoles and isothiocyanates). Swedes are low in calories.

Health benefits: fibre helps to stimulate regular bowel function and may protect against diseases of the digestive system, including cancer. Vitamin C is essential for the health of connective tissue, blood vessels, etc., promotes wound healing and may boost the immune system. It has antioxidant and anti-infective activity and may help to prevent viral infections such as the common cold. The phytochemicals in swedes continue to be the subject of detailed scientific research. Results suggest that these substances may act to protect the body against certain cancers, including breast cancer.

Cooking/serving methods: usually boiled and served as a mashed vegetable or diced and added to soups, stews, casseroles, etc.

Disadvantages: high consumption of the phytochemicals in swedes may interfere with iodine metabolism and increase the need to eat foods rich in this mineral, e.g. seafood.

Sweetbreads see **Offal**

Sweetcorn see **Corn**

Sweet potatoes see **Yams**

Tahini see **Sesame seeds**

Tangerines
Description: small, bright orange citrus fruits with sweet, juicy flesh containing numerous pips.

Properties: an excellent source of fruit sugar, fibre, vitamins (rich in C), minerals (including potassium) and bioflavonoids.

Health benefits: supply readily available energy. Soluble fibre helps to lower blood cholesterol levels and may protect against heart and circulatory disease. Insoluble fibre promotes regular bowel function and may help to prevent diseases of the digestive system, including cancer. Vitamin C is essential for the health of connective tissue, blood vessels, etc. It also promotes wound healing and may boost the immune system. It has anti-infective properties and may give some protection against viral infections such as the common cold. Vitamin C and bioflavonoids have antioxidant properties and are believed to reduce the risk of the occurrence of certain diseases, including some cancers.

Cooking/serving methods: usually eaten as fresh fruit and in fruit salad.

Disadvantages: numerous pips can lessen the appeal of tangerines for children.

Tarragon

Description: two varieties of this herb are known to have been cultivated for many centuries, one from Siberia and the other from southern Europe. Tarragon is mainly used for culinary purposes. It is less popular today as a herbal remedy than it was in the past.

Properties: contains a volatile oil and substances which confer a distinctive flavour.

Health benefits: formerly used in herbal medicine to stimulate the appetite and to cure toothache.

Cooking/serving methods: the fresh herb may be eaten in salads and tarragon is also used for dressings, flavoured vinegar and in pickles.

Disadvantages: usually none reported.

Tea

Description: one of the most popular drinks in Britain grown in India, Sri Lanka and China. In recent years, scientific studies have tended to suggest that there may be positive health benefits to be gained from drinking tea.

Properties: contains caffeine and bioflavonoids (including quercetin).

Health benefits: caffeine is a stimulant which can heighten alertness and increase heartbeat and respiration rate. Tea (especially green tea) contains natural antioxidants which may help to protect against certain cancers. Tea also has mild diuretic properties.

Cooking/serving methods: in Britain, most tea is drunk hot with added milk. Iced tea, with lemon or mint, is a refreshing alternative.

Disadvantages: if drunk excessively, tea can produce unpleasant symptoms such as insomnia, nervousness, etc. due to the presence of caffeine. It can also cause stomach irritation in people with ulcers and may trigger migraine in susceptible individuals. Tea can interfere with iron absorption, if taken in excess, and tannins in tea may stain teeth.

Thyme

Description: common or garden thyme is a popular, fragrant herb, cultivated throughout Britain. Used to flavour food and also for healing in herbal medicine.

Properties: contains a volatile oil and several active compounds.

Health benefits: in herbal medicine, the herb is administered as a fluid extract, infusion or volatile oil, usually with other remedies. It is used to ease respiratory symptoms of colds, flu, bronchitis, whooping cough and sinusitis. Thyme is administered to relieve indigestion and colic pains and as an antidote for mild depression.

Cooking/serving methods: fresh and dried thyme is used to flavour salads and many different savoury dishes.

Disadvantages: usually none reported.

Tofu see **Soya beans**

Tomatoes
Description: although more precisely fruits, tomatoes are

generally regarded, and used, as salad vegetables. Many different varieties are available, including some that are yellow rather than red. In Britain tomatoes are popular for greenhouse cultivation. They are also available tinned and concentrated as paste and tomato sauce.

Properties: an excellent source of vitamins (especially C and E), minerals (including potassium) and carotenoid pigments (lycopene).

Health benefits: provide valuable vitamins and minerals involved in essential metabolic functions and the maintenance of health. Vitamin C has anti-infective properties, promotes wound healing, may boost the immune system and help to ward off infections such as the common cold. Vitamins C and E and carotenoid pigments in tomatoes have antioxidant properties and may protect against some forms of cancer. Eating concentrated tomato paste or the ever-popular tomato ketchup has recently been found to be beneficial, especially for men, in helping to protect the prostate gland against disease.

Cooking/serving methods: may be eaten as fresh vegetables or used in cooking.

Disadvantages: rarely, may provoke allergy.

Tongue see **Offal**

Tripe see **Offal**

Trout

Description: oily, freshwater fish (although sea trout have a similar life cycle to salmon) of which there are three species in Britain. Sea trout are relatively large, silvery-coloured fish with pink flesh. Wild brown trout are usually smaller with coppery-brown, mottled colouring and pinkish buff-coloured flesh. Rainbow trout are a non-native, 'farmed' species with silvery spotted skin incorporating a variety of colours and pink flesh. This is the most widely available species on sale throughout the year.

Properties: an excellent source of protein, vitamins (Especially B_{12}, A and D), minerals (including iron) and essential omega-3 fatty acids.

Health benefits: supply first-class protein for tissue growth and repair. The vitamins and minerals contained in trout are required for various metabolic functions and for the maintenance of health of tissues and organs. Fish oils protect the heart and circulation and reduce the risk of development of diseases such as atherosclerosis, heart attack and stroke. Eating oily fish may improve the symptoms of psoriasis and arthritis. Omega-3 fatty acids are necessary for the development of the foetal brain and nervous system and pregnant women are advised to include oily fish in their diet.

Cooking/serving methods: may be grilled, baked or steamed and served with vegetables or salad.

Disadvantages: bones may be a choking hazard. Rarely, trout may cause allergy.

Tuna

Description: large, marine oily fish of which there are several species, imported into Britain. Previously only available in cans but now, increasingly, as fresh, pinky brown 'steaks' of dense flesh.

Properties: an excellent source of protein, vitamins (A, B_{12} and D), minerals (including iron) and essential omega-3 fatty acids.

Health benefits: provides first-class protein for tissue growth and repair. Vitamins and minerals contained in tuna are required for a number of metabolic functions and for the maintenance of health of tissues and organs. Fish oils protect the heart and circulation and reduce the risk of developing diseases such as atherosclerosis, heart attack and stroke. Eating oily fish may improve the symptoms of arthritis and psoriasis in some people. Omega-3 fatty acids are essential for the development of the foetal brain and nervous system, and pregnant women are advised to include oily fish in their diet.

Cooking/serving methods: baked, steamed, poached, grilled or incorporated into fish dishes.

Disadvantages: rarely, may cause allergy. Tinned tuna contains very little of the original fish oil which is removed during processing.

Turbot

Description: a brown, spotted flatfish with lumpy skin and white, delicately flavoured flesh. Sometimes available.

Properties: an excellent source of protein, vitamins (rich in B_{12}) and minerals (including iron and iodine). It is low in fat.

Health benefits: supplies protein for tissue growth and repair, and vitamins and minerals involved in essential metabolic functions and the maintenance of the health of tissues and organs.

Cooking/serving methods: may be poached, steamed, baked and/or incorporated into fish dishes.

Disadvantages: rarely, may cause allergy.

Turkey

Description: once only eaten at Christmas, turkey has become increasingly popular fare in supermarkets in recent years, in the form of 'steaks', diced and minced meat.

Properties: an excellent source of protein, vitamins (B_{12} and other B vitamins) and minerals (particularly phosphorus, potassium and zinc). White turkey (breast) meat is low in fat but the dark meat is a richer source of minerals. Most fat is unsaturated and located in the skin, which can be easily removed.

Health benefits: supplies first-class protein for tissue growth and repair, and vitamins and minerals that are involved in a range of metabolic functions and in maintenance of the health of tissues and organs.

Cooking/serving methods: whole turkeys are cooked by roasting. Supermarket cuts (usually of turkey breast) may be fried, roasted or cooked as ingredients of stews and casseroles.

Disadvantages: whole turkeys can be a source of food poisoning if not thoroughly cooked. Stuffing should be roasted separately and the bird cooked until the juices run clear and the meat separates easily from the bone.

Turmeric

Description: powdered, yellow spice used in Eastern cookery and for healing in traditional medicine.

Properties: contains various active substances and a natural dye.

Health benefits: in Eastern herbal medicine, turmeric is said to act as a tonic for the liver and to ease symptoms of inflammation. It is also used to treat indigestion and wind and to improve blood flow. Turmeric has mild antibacterial activity and may help in the treatment of infections.

Cooking/serving methods: used as a spice in curries and Eastern cookery.

Disadvantages: usually none reported.

Turnips

Description: round, pinkish white root vegetables with

white flesh, cultivated throughout Britain and also used for healing in herbal medicine. The leafy green tops can also be eaten as a vegetable.

Properties: an excellent source of fibre, vitamins (especially C) and minerals. The leaves contain vitamins A and C, iron and beta carotene (carotenes).

Health benefits: fibre promotes healthy bowel function and is believed to protect against diseases of the lower digestive system, including cancer. Vitamin C is essential for the health of connective tissue, blood vessels, etc. and promotes wound healing. It may support the immune system and has anti-infective properties, possibly helping to protect against viral infections such as the common cold. Vitamin C and beta carotene have powerful antioxidant activity and may protect against various diseases, including some cancers. In herbal medicine, turnips may be used to relieve chronic respiratory symptoms arising from infections, bronchitis and asthma.

Cooking/serving methods: usually boiled or steamed. They are often added to soups, stews and casseroles.

Disadvantages: usually none reported.

Ugli fruit (tangelo)

Description: unusual citrus fruit, which is a cross between a grapefruit and a tangerine. It has greenish-yellow, lumpy skin, sweet yellow flesh and is grapefruit-sized. Sometimes available.

Properties: an excellent source of fibre, vitamins (rich in C), minerals (including potassium) and flavonoids.

Health benefits: insoluble fibre promotes healthy bowel function and may help to protect against diseases, including some cancers, of the lower digestive system. Soluble fibre helps to lower blood cholesterol levels and may protect against heart and circulatory disease. Vitamins and minerals have many metabolic functions and are essential for the maintenance of health. Vitamin C and flavonoids have antioxidant properties and are believed to protect against a range of diseases, including some cancers. Vitamin C may also promote wound healing, boost the immune system and help to prevent common viral infections.

Cooking/serving methods: usually eaten as fresh fruit or as part of fruit salad.

Disadvantages: usually none reported.

Vanilla

Description: popular, sweet, fragrant flavouring derived from the pods of a tropical plant. Whole pods may be used but more often, a brown essence derived from them.

Properties: contains various active substances and a fragrant oil.

Health benefits: contains phytochemicals which may be beneficial.

Cooking/serving methods: used to flavour baked goods, e.g. cakes, biscuits and desserts.

Disadvantages: usually none reported.

Vegetable oils

Description: oils derived from the seeds, beans or nuts of a variety of different plants, including safflower, sesame seed, sunflower, soya, olive, rapeseed and walnut. (See individual entries.) They are good sources of vitamin E and unsaturated essential fatty acids and help the absorption of fat-soluble vitamins from the gut. Used in moderation, vegetable oils are considered to be beneficial to health but all are high in calories. In contrast to those listed above, palm oil and coconut oil contain mainly saturated fats, a high consumption of which has been linked to heart and circulatory disease.

Venison see **Game**

Vinegar

Description: sharp-tasting liquid, consisting mainly of water and acetic acid, which has long been used to preserve foods. Vinegar is produced by yeast fermentation in two stages. In addition to the familiar brown and white malt vinegars, there are many other varieties available. These include tarragon, balsamic, red wine, white wine and cider vinegars. The latter (made from the fermented juice of applies) is widely used for healing in naturopathy.

Properties: contains acetic acid and various other compounds and flavouring.

Health benefits: in naturopathy, cider vinegar (sometimes taken with honey) is believed to be beneficial in the relief of a number of different diseases and symptoms, including arthritis, digestive upsets and infections, diarrhoea and obesity, and is thought to act as a tonic for the liver.

Cooking/serving methods: sprinkled on foods to add flavour. Speciality vinegars are useful as low-calorie dressings for salads or to add flavour to cooked foods.

Disadvantages: may provoke allergic responses in some people.

Walnuts

Description: familiar, crinkly, brown nuts enclosed in hard, round shells that split easily into two halves along a natural seam. Walnut trees are grown in parts of Britain but most of the nuts are imported. They are used in home baking and in a wide range of manufactured foods, especially cakes, biscuits and desserts and are also available as pickled nuts.

Properties: a good source of protein for vegetarians (especially when combined with other vegetable proteins) and a rich source of unsaturated essential fatty acids. Excellent source of vitamins (especially B₁, B₃ and E) and minerals (particularly potassium iron, copper and phosphorus).

Health benefits: provide protein necessary for tissue growth and repair. Vitamins and minerals found in walnuts are involved in essential metabolic activities and the maintenance of health. Vitamin E has antioxidant activity and may help to prevent diseases, including some cancers. An American study suggested that eating 85 g (3 oz) of walnuts each day as part of an overall, low-fat diet, reduced levels of blood cholesterol and hence may protect against heart and circulatory disease. Essential fatty acids in walnuts are involved in complex processes and are necessary for health. In herbal medicine, walnut vinegar (from pickled walnuts) is prescribed as a gargle for sore or ulcerated throats and the leaves and bark are also used as remedies for healing.

Cooking/serving methods: may be eaten as whole nuts or used chopped in baking, desserts or in savoury dishes and salads.

Disadvantages: high in calories. They may be a potential choking hazard and can provoke allergy.

Water

The human body is largely made up of water, which comprises about 60 per cent of the overall mass. It must be continuously replenished as it is constantly being used and lost. Natural loss occurs through the processes of urination, respiration and sweating but water is involved in nearly all metabolic processes. An average adult requires about three litres of water each day, depending upon body size and weight. Most of this needs to be obtained by drinking (62 per cent) while the remainder is supplied from the water content of food, with a small amount generated by metabolic processes.

Water is so essential that human beings quickly die, within a matter of a few days, if they are deprived of it. Health experts recommend drinking six to eight glasses of plain water each day, along with other drinks, to ensure an adequate intake of fluid. It is estimated that many people do not drink enough and are consequently slightly dehydrated for much of the time. This can cause symptoms such as headache, irritability and forgetfulness. It can put a strain on the kidneys and increase the risk of urinary tract infections and kidney stones. In older age, the sensation of thirst can diminish and hence the elderly are at particular risk of dehydration, as are small children. In the event of a urinary tract infection, drinking plenty of water helps to flush out the causative organisms and promotes healing. Drinking plenty of water, especially in frequent sips, is vitally important for anyone suffering from a bout of sickness or diarrhoea, when dehydration poses a particular risk.

Many people are worried about chemical additives and pollutants that may be present in mains water supplies (although water quality is subject to rigorous monitoring). Water filters and other purification systems have become increasingly popular in recent years, which can remove compounds, including minerals which may be beneficial to health. Bottled waters are a widely available and popular alternative and many people prefer the taste of these to their own tap water. However, although bottled and 'mineral' waters are safe to drink, they are not necessarily free of compounds and additives. When travelling abroad in countries where the quality of water may be suspect, it is essential to boil water, use purification tablets or to drink bottled water to guard against the risk of disease.

Watercress

Description: the green stems and leaves of watercress have a slightly 'hot' flavour and are excellent in salads. Watercress has been recognized as one of a group of (cruciferous) vegetables that are believed to reduce the risk of some cancers, if eaten on a regular basis. Watercress grows in or near fresh water and is cultivated in Britain. It has been valued for centuries by herbalists for its healing properties.

Properties: an excellent source of vitamins (A, C and E) and minerals (Iron, calcium magnesium) and beta carotene (carotenes). Has natural antibiotic properties.

Health benefits: contains vitamins and minerals that are involved in vital metabolic processes and are essential for the health of tissues and organs. Research indicates that regular consumption of watercress reduces the risk of the occurrence of certain cancers including those of the lower digestive system and bladder. In herbal medicine, watercress has been used to treat tuberculosis, bronchitis and coughs and as a stimulant for the digestive system. It is also used to stimulate the removal of toxic wastes from the tissues and blood and to treat urinary tract infections. The leaves are used as a poultice to treat arthritis and gout and the extracted juice is said to clear up spots and minor skin problems. Chewing the leaves is said to strengthen the gums.

Cooking/serving methods: served as a salad vegetable.

Disadvantages: wild watercress should not be gathered as a species of tiny snail that lives on the plant harbours parasitic liver flukes that can be passed on to people. There is also a risk of bacterial contamination (listeriosis). Watercress should be purchased from a reliable, controlled source and washed in clean running water before use.

Watermelon
Description: large melons with green rind and bright red, juicy, sweetish flesh studded with black seeds.
Properties: an excellent source of fluid. It contains some vitamin C and traces of other nutrients, including beta carotene. It is low in calories.
Health benefits: the main benefit of watermelon is its refreshing thirst-quenching quality. It also supplies traces of useful vitamins and minerals.
Cooking/serving methods: usually eaten as it is, cut into slices.
Disadvantages: usually none reported.

Wheat
Description: staple cereal crop in Britain, used to make flour for bread and many other foods. Wheat-based products are most nutritious when they are derived from the whole grain, including bran. Many wheat flours are highly refined and processed and may have nutrients added at a later stage. Wheat contains gluten and is defined as hard or soft, depending upon the actual amount in the different varieties of the cereal. Durum wheat is the hardest, with the highest gluten content. Ground coarse durum wheat is semolina, which is used in many ways in savoury and dessert cookery. Durum wheat flour is used to make the many different forms of pasta popular in recent years, e.g. macaroni and cannelloni.
Properties: an excellent source of protein, starch, vitamins (especially B group and E), minerals (including iron and calcium) and fibre.
Health benefits (wholewheat): a useful source of protein

for vegetarians (especially if eaten with other vegetable proteins) for tissue growth and repair. It also supplies vitamins and minerals involved in metabolic processes and essential for health. Wholewheat provides slow-release energy, avoiding peaks of blood glucose, and is therefore helpful in the control and possible prevention of diabetes. Fibre promotes healthy bowel function and may help to prevent diseases of the lower digestive system, including cancer.

Cooking/serving methods: wheat flour is used in a wide variety of ways, for bread, baked goods, etc. Grains, wheat flakes, etc. are used in breakfast cereals. Pasta, spaghetti, noodles, semolina, cous cous and whole dried wheat grains (cooked and served like rice) are other wheat products.

Disadvantages: not suitable for people with gluten intolerance or coeliac disease. Wheat bran interferes with the absorption of some nutrients, if eaten excessively. Also, it can act as an irritant to the digestive system in susceptible people and may exacerbate certain disorders such as colitis and irritable bowel syndrome.

Whelks

Description: shellfish with pointed, brownish buff shells harvested from shores around the British Isles. They are usually sold boiled and shelled.

Properties: a good source of protein, vitamins (especially B_{12} and E) and minerals (particularly copper and zinc).

Health benefits: supply first-class protein for tissue growth and repair and vitamins and minerals involved in metabolic functions and in maintaining health.

Cooking/serving methods: usually eaten sprinkled with vinegar on toast.

Disadvantages: like all shellfish, they may provoke allergy and are a potential source of food poisoning since they are vulnerable to bacterial contamination. Whelks should always be eaten fresh or as soon after purchase as possible.

White fish
Description: many marine fish species of two basic types – round-bodied and flatfish. They include cod, haddock, whiting, skate and sole (see individual entries). All are excellent sources of first-class protein, vitamins (especially B_{12}) and minerals (including iron) and are very low in fat.

Whiting
Description: a popular, round, marine fish with silvery, olive-brown skin and white flesh. It is sold in fishmongers and used in many manufactured fish dishes.
Properties: an excellent source of protein, vitamins (especially B_{12}) and minerals (including iron). It is very low in fat.
Health benefits: provides first-class protein for tissue growth and repair, and vitamins and minerals which are essential for health.
Cooking/serving methods: may be poached, baked, steamed or fried and served as main course or incorporated into fish dishes.
Disadvantages: rarely, may cause allergy. Fish bones can be a choking hazard.

Wild rice
Description: not a true rice but long, thin, blackish seeds of a wild grass that grows in wetlands in North America.
Properties: a good source of starch, vitamins (rich in B group but not B_{12}) and minerals.

Winkles

Health benefits: provides slow-release energy, avoiding peaks of blood glucose, and is therefore useful in the control and treatment of diabetes. B vitamins are involved in many metabolic functions and in the maintenance of health of tissues and organs.

Cooking/serving methods: often cooked and served with white rice, such as basmati, and used in hot and cold savoury dishes.

Disadvantages: usually none reported.

Winkles

Description: small, black-shelled shellfish. They are harvested around British coasts and usually sold ready boiled in the shell.

Properties: an excellent source of protein, vitamins (especially B group) and minerals (including zinc, selenium, iodine, iron, magnesium and calcium). They contain small amounts of omega-3 fatty acids.

Health benefits: supply first-class protein for tissue growth and repair, and vitamins and minerals involved in a range of metabolic functions and the maintenance of health.

Cooking/serving methods: traditionally 'winkled' out from their shells with a pin and served, sprinkled with vinegar, on toast.

Disadvantages: like all shellfish, a fairly common cause of allergy and food poisoning. They should be purchased from a reliable source and eaten very fresh.

Yams (sweet potatoes)

Description: exotic vegetables of two different types, either elongated or rounded, usually with pinkish purple skin. One type has creamy-coloured flesh and in the other is more orange coloured. The flesh has a markedly sweet flavour.

Properties: an excellent source of starch, vitamins (especially C), minerals (including potassium) and the orange-fleshed type are rich in beta carotene.

Health benefits: provide slow-release energy, avoiding peaks of blood glucose, and are therefore useful for the control and possible prevention of diabetes. Yams supply vitamins and minerals that are involved in essential metabolic functions and the maintenance of health. Vitamin C and beta carotene have powerful antioxidant properties and may help to prevent diseases, including cancer. Vitamin C has anti-infective properties, promotes wound healing and may boost the immune system. It also may help to prevent common viral infections such as colds.

Cooking/serving methods: usually scrubbed or peeled, cooked by boiling and served in the same way as potatoes.

Disadvantages: usually none reported.

Yeast extract

Description: familiar, brown, savoury spread, available as a manufactured product in jars.

Properties: an excellent source of B vitamins and minerals. It is low in calories.

Health benefits: a concentrated source of vitamins and minerals that are involved in many metabolic functions and in the maintenance of health.

Cooking/serving methods: usually eaten spread thinly on toast, bread or savoury biscuits.

Disadvantages: most extracts have a high salt content and may not be suitable for people with high blood pressure, heart problems or those on low sodium diets.

Yoghurt

Description: made by the action of bacteria on milk, plain

Yoghurt

and flavoured yoghurts have become extremely popular as dessert and snack foods. There are numerous varieties available, most made from cows' milk, although Greek yoghurt is derived from ewes' milk. Bio and live yoghurts contain bacterial cultures which are said to have particular health benefits. However, most yoghurts contain live bacteria.

Properties: a good source of protein, vitamins (especially B_2 and B_{12}) and minerals (particularly calcium and phosphorus). Yoghurt may be low or high in fat, depending on the variety.

Health benefits: provides protein for tissue growth and repair, and vitamins and minerals that are involved in the maintenance of good health. Calcium and phosphorus are essential for strong bones and teeth. Yoghurt can help to restore the bacterial flora of the gut after debilitating illness and it may be beneficial to people suffering from a range of other illnesses. It is easy to digest and useful in convalescence.

Cooking/serving methods: may be eaten as it is or added to both savoury and sweet cooked dishes.

Disadvantages: usually none reported.

Build Your Argument